SEARCH NEW PROFITS

How U.S. SMB and Startup Succeed in Emerging Markets

Stephan S Sunn

Davidson Global Partners, LLC

Copyright © 2024 Stephan S. Sunn

Disclaimer:

This book may not be reproduced or transmitted in any form without the written permission of the authors. Every effort has been made to make this guide as complete and accurate as possible. Although the authors have prepared this guide with the greatest of care, and have made every effort to ensure its accuracy, we assume no responsibility or liability for errors, inaccuracies, or omissions. Before you begin, check with the appropriate authorities to ensure compliance with all laws and regulations. Every effort has been made to make this report as complete and accurate as possible. However, there may be mistakes in typography or content. Also, this report contains information on online marketing and technology only up to the publishing date. Therefore, this report should be used as a guide – not as the ultimate source of Internet marketing information. The purpose of this report is to educate. The authors do not warrant that the information contained in this report is fully complete and shall not be responsible for any errors or omissions. The authors shall have neither liability nor responsibility to any person or entity concerning any loss or damage caused or alleged to be caused directly or indirectly by this report, nor do we make any claims or promises of our ability to generate income by using any of this information.

Davidsons Global Partners & Co. LLC, Davidson, NC 28036, USA; All Inquiries of copyrights, and cooperation go to: Stephan.sunn@aya.yale.edu

PREFACE

The author of this book series and their partners possess over 20 years of experience in their respective fields. They are widely recognized and respected within their professional communities and international networks. Prior to the pandemic, this group would convene at least once a year at locations around the globe. We were grateful to be healthy when we met for the first time after that global catastrophe.

When we resumed meeting, the realization that life is fragile and fleeting prompted an idea about the merits of documenting our work, successes or failures, so our colleagues now and future could benefit from it. With the 2022 arrival of ChatGPT and other groundbreaking AI technologies, we concurred on the urgency to expedite this documentation before such innovations fundamentally transform our lives and society, akin to the impact of COVID-19.

This book series focuses on the business domains in which we have supported clients worldwide last two decades. While the structure may not adhere to academically logical or analytically procedural norms, each major section evidences its importance in increasing the probability of success, enhancing production efficiency, or improving return on investment. Each book culminates with a "Chapter of Lessons" that summarizes some of the frequently encountered pitfalls in our practices. For privacy and confidentiality, public examples illustrate these lessons.

While advising numerous Fortune 500 companies and enterprises on international growth and market expansion strategies, the author has also realized the vast opportunities and unique challenges that emerging markets present for US-based small and medium businesses (SMBs) and startup companies. Large multinational corporations have established processes for tapping into new geographic markets, but smaller companies often lack the resources, experience, and strategic guidance to effectively identify, enter, and capitalize on high-growth emerging market opportunities.

Driven by this realization, the author's motivation is to provide a comprehensive playbook tailored specifically to US SMBs and startups seeking to expand their reach and revenue streams into emerging economies. By leveraging over two decades of real-world consulting insights from working with American companies of all sizes, one of the book's main objectives is demystifying the process.

From analyzing market potential and navigating regulatory landscapes to structuring partnerships and executing best practices, the author's mission is to level the playing field, allowing ambitious US businesses to confidently venture beyond domestic borders and access the immense growth prospects that the world's emerging markets provide.

EXECUTIVE SUMMARY

In the current turbulent global market and domestic uncertainties, emerging markets provide American SMBs and startups with incredible growth opportunities. They also pose unique challenges obviously. This semi-analytical, semi-prescriptive handbook is designed to help American SMBs and entrepreneurs thrive in fast-growing new markets. Conversely, governments, technology parks, and corporations in emerging countries can use this book to learn how to partner with US companies in their markets for their customers. The themes of this book are:

- Research and Identify Matching Market(s)
- Choose Market Entry Mode
- Local Marketing and Sales Tactics
- Managing risk effectively
- Become Active and Reputable in the Local Market
- Risk Detection and Control
- Fully Legal Compliant
- Don't Involve the Politics in Destinations
- Talent Search and Retention
- Balance of Standardization and Localization

"The Lessons" is the last Chapter of this book. It comesfrom our decades-long business practices. The readers might have their own opinions on the same topics. Different perspectives on this important topic expand the spectrum of the knowledge the leaders of US SMBs or startups could benefit. This is a good thing.

Penetrating foreign markets is challenging but ultimately profitable, and U.S. enterprises stand a fair chance by making profits from much larger and fast-growing new territories.

Objectives of this Book

Assist small and medium-sized businesses and entrepreneurs in studying, entering, and succeeding in growing markets around the world. The goals are:

1. Determine appealing possibilities in developing locations through market evaluations
2. Offer useful approaches to enter the market, such as customizing products to local preferences, forming alliances, and connecting with those who have a vested interest in the market
3. Assistance navigating operational, cultural, and ethical obstacles
4. Offer strategies to remain competitive with domestic rivals and conglomerates.
5. Prepare leaders to adjust products, messages and leadership.

CHAPTER 1: WHY EMERGING MARKETS

Potential of Emerging Markets for U.S. SMEs and Startups

American small and mid-size companies and startup companies could benefit from entering markets in emerging countries. In 2023 the International Monetary Fund or IMF predicts that emerging economies will grow 4.7%, faster than already developed economies[1].

Development in these areas is stimulated by rapid urbanization and a rising middle class. By 2025, the world's middle class will total 3.2 billion, 88% of them in Asia, according to Brookings[2]. Underbanked consumers with greater disposable income offer enormous market potential for local goods, fashion, ready meals, personal care items, electronics, and tourism[3].

The same digital revolution is happening in Indonesia, Nigeria, and India, where internet and smartphone usage are exploding. Internet penetration in Indonesia doubled from 30% in 2015 to 63% in 2021. Platforms such as Tokopedia and GoPay are examples of innovative business models made possible by increased connectivity and computer literacy. U.S. small and start-up businesses with IT expertise could take advantage of the digital age by providing digital solutions in cloud computing, cyber security, online education, telemedicine, and financial services.

The hospitality business, for example, is experimenting with commercial model innovations to address the lack of availability, accessibility, and/or affordability of clean water and energy. Other domestic industries are also addressing these innovation opportunities: agriculture, education, and more. Some of these emerging innovations may diffuse globally with further refinement and scale. U.S. companies will acquire developing market IP through acquisition, joint ventures, and licensing.

Traceable AI, an AI start-up that spots fakes in fast-growing markets, has seen some big wins. By using new technology to tackle a local issue, Traceable has won clients including the Central Bank of Nigeria, Bank of Mexichem, and Bank of Brasil companies in banking, pharma and chemicals. IT consulting firm DCX Technology Partners looked to Indonesian unicorn GoTo as its entry point for expansion.

Attractiveness of the New Markets:

1. Expanding markets of customers for goods and services.
2. Mobile and internet access were increased, as so digital business models.
3. Fast-growing number of middle-class citizens and faster-growing young consumers.
4. Increasing disposable income and the willingness of consumers to spend.
5. Reduced levels of competitiveness result in unique value propositions for U.S. brands.
6. Investments are increased in public and private infrastructure and technology verticals
7. Stronger interests in innovations and IPs
8. Stronger economic ties between the U.S. and emerging countries

Obstacles facing American Enterprises:

Despite their efforts, small and medium-sized businesses (SMBs) and entrepreneurs in the United States still confront obstacles to entering foreign markets. The U.S. Small Business Administration (SBA) finds that 63 percent of SMBs said financial and human resources restrict their ability to achieve foreign growth [4]. Most smaller firms lack working capital and cash flow to undertake growth, let alone internationalization.

The radius of expansion diversity multiplies problems. NSBA research finds that 72 percent of small businesses struggle with foreign regulations and market developments. Every region presents different consumer preferences; culture, legal, and political contexts; and infrastructural reliability issues. Problems could, for example, relate to limits on foreign ownership and profit repatriation, or local business registration.

SMB leadership teams may face ethical challenges with corruption, unethical conduct, cyber risks, and IP protection. Global-scale multinationals have advantages in brand equity, scale, local knowledge, and regulatory relationships that smaller U.S. companies can't match. Some markets contain numerous government hurdles.

The main obstacles include:

1. Constraints on capital, time, and management bandwidth
2. Lack of knowledge about different cultural and regulatory conditions
3. Not enough knowledgeable international HR with an understanding of local culture
4. Some countries experience political instability and economic chaos
5. Deficiencies in infrastructure, connectivity, and utilities
6. Unethical Business Operations, Corruption; No Full Protection of Intellectual Property.
7. Uncertainty regarding currency exchange rates

Conquering Challenges

SMBs entering Latin America, Southeast Asia, or beyond have seized these challenges with preparedness, adaptation, and strong alliances [5]. For example, digital channels provide market research and high-potential opportunity discovery from anywhere. HubSpot and Zendesk make customer preferences and local presence easier.

Growth money is now accessible via crowdfunding; For example, www.Export.gov offers training, contacts, and finance. Exports, e-commerce, and licensing all support start-ups exploring markets with iterative resource commitment. Knowledge transfer happens through local corporations, accelerators, and multilateral institution alliances.

Cultural training, local advisory teams, and immersion build market fluency. Strong founder monitoring, financial controls, and ethics keep corruption in check. Emerging markets could revitalize US SMB innovation with resilience, adaptation, and devotion.

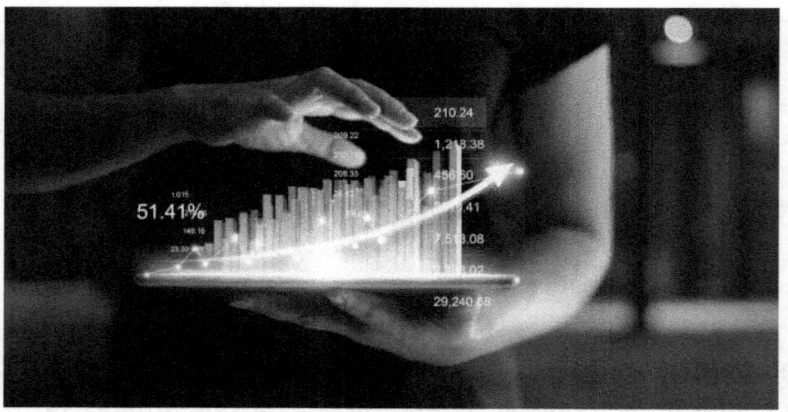

CHAPTER 2: GLOBAL MARKET LANDSCAPE

Define 'Emerging Markets'

An emerging market is a fast-growing, industrializing economy. Under their promise and increasing global integration, these low-income to middle-income nations are important to the global economy. Emerging markets share common characteristics such as:

1. A big, young population can harness the power of the workforce and consumer growth, which manufacturing a major economic driver.
2. Urbanization patterns hasten migration from the countryside to cities, producing megacities and hubs of innovation and consumption.
3. A more generous middle class, with more disposable income than ever, elevates demand across industries.
4. Industrial underdevelopment and poor infrastructure; other regions are less advanced.
5. Heightened trade, foreign investment and adoption of new technology to spur development. However, this leaves them more exposed to global economic shocks.
6. Political turmoil, regulatory uncertainty and economic turbulence are downsides. Yet judicious companies could profit from rapid growth.

Current Global Economic Trends

Currently, some crucial principles impact the economy on a worldwide scale. The key portion of economic expansion is as of now stemming from menaces that are prudently and painstakingly developing in those specific areas such as Asia, Africa, the Middle East, and Latin America. That is, they are the outskirts of the classic developed world. And global growth, while weakened, is expected to continue to be driven by the emerging world.

The increased interconnectedness of markets and supply chains brought by globalization has significantly enhanced access to global markets. The backlash of growing nationalism and protectionism is increasingly impeding global investment and commerce. The world community struggles to figure out just where they want to draw the lines. At the same time, a growing concern about sustainability among investors and customers is compelling more firms than ever to think out of the box and adopt practices that are more in harmony with the green themes that consumers and shareholders alike prize. That tendency might be most noticeable in the developing market.

The international economy is going through a demographic transformation, in which most industrialized economies are struggling with aging societies while developing countries are facing a youth bulge. These transitional phases are likely to affect consumption, labor markets, and growth prospects. Service industries, like information technology, healthcare, education, and tourism, are booming in the developing world.

Volatility in financial markets due to geopolitical conflicts, economic policies, and global catastrophes such as pandemics creates a state of uncertainty. Rapid urbanization creates areas of high economic activity and innovation, which attract business investment, human capital, and informal economic activity, as well as issuing challenges of pollution, congestion, and infrastructural pressure.

How Technological and Socioeconomic Factors Affect Market Terrains

Markets in Emerging Countries Formed by Urbanization and Growth of Megacities

1. Urbanization and the growth of megacities concentrate on the demand for commercial and technological goods and services.

2. The Rising middle class demands a broader range of consumer products and services, including banking, transportation, healthcare, and education.
3. Young, digitally active populations embrace mobile payments, e-commerce, and social networking.
4. Investment in infrastructure, including highways, electricity grids, and commercial real estate, needed to support growing urbanization and industrialization.
5. Emerging nations often bypass traditional stages of growth in areas such as digital banking (mobile money), e-commerce, and the sharing economy, thanks to technology leapfrogging.
6. Stronger and closer ties of emerging markets with global value chains, commerce, investment, and businesses; Meanwhile, developing countries are more vulnerable to global market downturns.

Misunderstandings about Emerging Markets are Widespread

1. Instead of assessing the intricacies and diversity in emerging markets, we could assume that everything is high-risk; it's an easy out. Certainly, there are significant day-to-day risks in some of these markets, but proper management and assessment can produce a world of opportunities.
2. In the minds of many marketers, it is believed that consumers in fast-growing markets have low purchasing power and prefer cheap products. However, the purchasing power of the middle classes is rising, and they are driving growth in both the value and premium segments in fast-growing markets.
3. Misguided idea about less-developed business environments. Many multinationals have been successful in these contemporary, infrastructure-laden economies.
4. Assuming that the extent of bribery and corruption is quite high. In reality, the majority of business is ethical. And governments are beginning to shift toward better governance.
5. The returns may be unpredictable – but the upside development potential in emerging nations outweighs that in mature ones.

6. Presuming Western products and services are loved by developing countries. Actually, local goods and brands are finding more favor with consumers, not to mention the quality products from the other developing countries.
7. Unaware of the local markets' innovations and technology services.

Emerging Markets Use More Technologies Today Than Before

1. Because of the prevalent utilization of the internet and people increasingly depending on their cell phones, trades become digital. People no longer use simple phones, but have multiplied their dependence on smartphones.
2. The demand for fintech, digital payments, cryptocurrencies, and online loans is growing and helping to include people who previously could not get access to the banking system in our financial infrastructure.
3. The demands of e-commerce and online services continue to grow due to an aging population, a rising middle class, and logistics.
4. Updating processes at companies requires technologies such as cloud computing, artificial intelligence, big data analytics, the Internet of Things, IoT, 3-D printing and so on in today's digital age.
5. It is nearly essential for sharing services to be integrated with rides and bikes in densely populated cities.

Advice for SMBs and startups in America:

1. Leverage strong growth rates and growing customer demand by customizing and acknowledging different tastes. One-size-fits-all just doesn't cut it.
2. Working together with local businesses can be an effective way to deal with the obstacles of market restrictions and red tape.

Furthermore, showing respect for the local culture can go a long way to establishing rapport and creating trust.
3. In some areas, the adoption of novel technology and innovations may give an edge. Swift adaptation of tech makes room for contemporary solutions.
4. Striking a balance between risk and return is crucial. With careful thought, possibilities will outweigh the challenges of diverse, fast-changing, and complex circumstances.
5. Joining the ranks of international markets by way of value chains and trade flows is useful, and necessitates supply chain resilience in the face of shocks.

The data and news illustrate that emerging markets are dynamic, hold tremendous growth potential and require specific strategies. To succeed in engaging with these countries, the ability to keep up with the speed of change and to build relationships as markets evolve is essential. By applying the right strategy emerging markets may provide a driver of global corporate growth for decades to come.

CHAPTER 3: CHALLENGES TO U.S. SMBS AND STARTUPS

Challenges SMEs Face In the US Market.

For SMBs and startups, the US market is an obstacle course for trying to build and scale, despite being the largest economy. That's because entrenched large companies with vast resources make it exceptionally hard to find and keep a niche in most sectors, especially. The competition is especially deadly in saturated industries with hundreds of participants and minimal differentiation. In retail, for example, market leaders like Walmart and Amazon are ravenously defending their places, so getting onto the shelf and into the trial is increasingly difficult for newer brands.

Industries such as automotive and tech are also dominated by goliaths able to leverage their scale and multi-billion war chests. Tiny startups battle for limited elbow room amid a Big Three in Detroit or Silicon Valley titans like Google and Apple, despite superior innovations. Large incumbents tilt market dynamics further by lobbying pliable policy-makers. High real estate rentals, wage rates and operations costs also combine to make the U.S. an expensive market to do business in, which severely erodes the margins of the smaller enterprises struggling to stay afloat.

It remains arduous and pricey for newcomers to secure and sustain selective domestic customers, with innumerable options for goods and services. Their demands for ease, customization, and brand thrills rise ever higher while their dedication erodes. For SMBs, prosperity lies less in getting the basics right than in getting posts to go viral. The very possibility of survival turns on access to angel funds, not validated value propositions.

Basically, the economic factors for smaller U.S. companies are making success in the domestic markets look like a cruel, congested 'red ocean' with eroding profit pools and frenzied consolidation that advantage bigger sharks. Most start-ups continue to be severely disadvantaged in efforts to stay truly differentiated.

Embrace Diversification to Defy Economic Uncertainty

Given the inherent challenges startups and SMBs face in their domestic markets, spreading your presence across various emerging regions becomes imperative. This is especially true whenever signs of cyclical downturns in the US appear. Of late, the pandemic accentuated the vulnerability of just relying on the home turf.

Diversifying operations among various emerging markets is important because it lessens exposure to risks specific to certain localities, like demand downturns or policy shocks. Latin America's business cycles, for example, seldom mimic North America's. So a global customer base guarantees steadier revenue flows, which can act as inoculation against domestic recessions.

By and large, emerging markets deliver higher GDP growth rates than developed ones, which project a wealth of greenfield expansion prospects. Their burgeoning consumer classes comprise demographics on the rise economically, willing to trade up to premium indulgences and lifestyle upgrades. That makes these territories inviting habitats for U.S. corporations striving to achieve category primacy in nascent segments where rivals are usually less advanced.

Emerging regions also allow for testing new offerings, tech, or business designs at scale. You keep control of operating expenses by employing property and even capability overseas. You benefit from localized partnerships for pivotal distribution leverage and feet-on-street access to remote customer segments. Regulatory matches for sustainability, industrial development, or infrastructure projects can catalyze whole sector-wide expansions.

Having early experiences with different regional legislations, cultures and ways of "doing business" also prepares the startups for later global expansion. Their successful experiments with select EMs as "test beds" provide room for fine-tuning their expansion playbooks, and to build organizational resilience.

American Products and Solutions are Welcome in Emerging Markets.

Although American startups grapple with a surfeit of obstacles in domestic markets across most timeworn industries, they nonetheless wield a special advantage in technology sectors thanks to innovation pipelines and first-rate research and development infrastructure. We're not just talking monopolies in Silicon Valley. Plenty of emerging markets still have deficiencies of access, affordability, or both in today's leading technologies, products, and services, including everything from AI and cloud tools to fintech apps, IoT devices, EVs, e-health platforms, agritech solutions, enterprise solutions, and much more.

There is rapid adoption of digital transformation initiatives across the government departments in large public sector utilities like education, healthcare, energy, mobility, logistics, etc. as a key requirement for realizing several national priorities around uplifting standards of living, delivering citizen services, improving infrastructure, etc., where US technological solutions have a unique capability for driving a disruptive change. For example, nurturing the digital economy ecosystem that includes mitigating risks around data privacy, cybersecurity, etc. can be achieved by technologists leveraging emerging technologies such as Blockchain. Similarly, strengthening medical infrastructure and combating talent shortages in healthcare delivery, especially in remote villages remain a stumbling block to most nations' quest for universal health coverage goals, where our innovators showcase a host of telehealth and mHealth platforms that close these acute shortages of medical services in remote villages by directly connecting these distant patients to specialist physician networks through digital channels.

The distinct technology segments that are witnessing rising demand in the developing markets are – fintech, agritech, healthtech, edutech, e-commerce, smart mobility, and much more. Clearly, the U.S. companies, big or SMEs, ruling these domains globally are the most dynamically positioned entities to penetrate these regions. The U.S. has only a 5% smartphone penetration as compared to the developed markets of Japan and Korea. However, 73% of this demographic is projected to own smartphones by 2020, according to GSMA. Simply put, with platforms already developed for Western customers, U.S. firms can plug and play their way into billions-strong markets.

Risks of Being Small and New - "Red Ocean"

In America, a vast array of products and services from all over the world flood the market. While consumers are relishing the global selections in this most dynamic economy, the sad fact concerning the U.S. marketplace is that the competition levels today are tantamount to dogfights in most fields controlled by market-leading behemoths – thus allowing virtually no breathing space for newcomers to exist and prosper significantly without lifelines from outsiders.

The automotive industry is still very much in thrall to Detroit's "Big Three" despite Tesla's valiant forays. Tech is still the fiefdom of the FAANG giants that startups develop inferiority complexes off of. Even consumer goods categories have entrenched empires—P&G, J&J, Coke, and Pepsi—that lord over shelf space in retail and mindshare across generations of consumers. But beyond the flagrant cases, every niche has market leaders whose bulwarks are under siege from newcomers.

For startups barking at the edges, success relies too heavily on virality and influencer marketing instead of product quality or distribution. Profitability remains elusive as companies depend on discount economics and negative gross margin business models to acquire customers. Survival is merely an exercise in extending the runway from venture capitalists instead of charting paths to self-sustainability.

Incumbent heavyweights' sheer intensity of activity along two different dimensions to simultaneously woo customers through massive advertising and lobby policymakers through muscle power renders the operating environment daunting for smaller, younger firms lacking such resources. In ever-shrinking contestable markets, ultimately, domestic territory in recent times has come to resemble intensely contested 'red oceans' where outcompeting the fortified defenses of incumbent corporate powers without their enterprise budgets remains a near-impossibility at scale for most start-ups.

Embracing a "Blue Ocean Strategy"

Unlike the dangerous "red oceans" in the United States, emerging markets outside of the country resemble "blue oceans". In these markets, potentially lucrative opportunities exist because, although they are known to multinationals, large pools of dormant demand are still untapped by Western hegemonic corporations. As relatively embattled local champions continue to reinvent themselves, vast new segments of increasingly affluent customers are also coming online.

In the case of U.S. companies especially in verticals such as tech, these near-virgin markets with close to 700 million middle-class households are rich soils for organically co-building brands with partners and users, and in developing regions they offer the chance to achieve product-market fit faster at more measurable customer acquisition costs than exorbitant advertising spends in saturated home categories. Willingness to pay remains higher for world-class solutions addressing accessibility gaps.

In order to achieve a more massive scale economically and societally, next-gen innovators need to adopt a blended philosophy of glocalization for user needs and best practices around integrity, governance and impact for large-scale principles. The latter ensures sustainable operations. Fit-for-purpose micro solutions for unique consumer problems can drive organic adoption and retention. National priority-driven policy incentives and strategic partnerships with progressive national and local governments looking to improve life for their citizens and turn around their economies can lead to the whole market building.

Fundamentally, neglected emerging markets abroad nowadays represent American tech outfits' 'blue ocean' chances to capture initial customer and market share leads and gain premium expansion paths ahead while eventual domestic saturation curtails.

When put in a nutshell, smaller businesses and younger startups still have multiple battles to fight just to get traction against entrenched incumbents across industries, even despite America's massive, scalable market. Domestically, the market realities more and more look like cutthroat "red oceans," with constrained paths for emerging successfully without huge capital reserves well out of proportion to the total addressed market size.

It is wise to spread your money out all over the world to reduce risk. But in some developing regions, there's still plenty of "blue ocean" yet to be traversed, creating an abundance of opportunities. Early entry into these regions can help a start-up learn strategic playbooks, gain insights, and build relationships. If customize products or services to meet local markets, respect local culture and regulations, and build a great team, the US SME and startup can build a business for international success before there is limited room to grow domestically.

CHAPTER 4: SEARCH PROFITABLE MARKETS

The right choice of international markets to enter can make or break the success of the global expansion of U.S. SMBs and startups. Extensive research should drive the selection, based on quantitative data and qualitative insights of addressable market sizes, growth trends, competitive forces at play, regulatory climate, socio-political stability, ease of doing business, and cultural fit. Indexing target countries and segments to construct a portfolio ensures systematic evaluation.

Compile Portfolios of Different Markets

To organize a portfolio of emerging markets, U.S. companies should rate key emerging regions against important parameters that can be used to compare options. In a portfolio, countries are tracked across key business environment metrics like GDP growth, per capita income, consumer spending, quality of infrastructure, technology adoption rates, quality and availability of skill pool, and degree of government support. Additionally, countries can be tracked for parameter ease/cost of company incorporation, taxation regime, and legal enforceability as their impact on operational overheads is a large one.

After measuring how well-emerging markets perform in these three dimensions, there are clear leaders. India and Indonesia come first in tech talent and scale. Mexico and Brazil score higher in manufacturing abilities. Singapore and UAE set up the easiest: They provide the most business-friendly bureaucracies. South Africa and Nigeria look the most promising in consumer sectors. The "best" outcome depends on your business's priorities. If you want to tap technical competencies, choose from the tech talent group. If you want to benefit from incentives, choose from the bureaucratic group.

Granular market segmentation would extend to profiling sub-segments within countries by growth rates, levels of competition, and complexities matching and enhancing distribution strengths. Weighted scoring locates the most accessible and higher potential sub-segments for primary attention. If global peers have prospering models for attacking such niches locally, their success validates the commerciality of given openings. The country + sub-segment combination that yields the best index scores is identified as the most promising beachhead market for initial inroads.

In a constantly changing global market, small- and medium-sized businesses and startups in the United States must examine their market placement in a thoughtful manner. This involves pinpointing a variety of market placements with diverse levels of maturation and potential. For instance, a technological startup may test efficient placements like South Korea for technology adoption right away and also strive to expand into protoplast markets such as Brazil, where the technological dais is undergoing instant development.

Rank Locations with Potential Sizes and Growth Rates

In comparison to developed nations, broader developing regions are forecasted to have higher growth paths, although there is a huge difference among specific nation members in all of these regions. Consumer bases are growing faster, according to fine market analyses.

India, for instance, leads the rise in Gross National Income (GNI) among the BRICS bunch with 7% growth, on a sturdy 1.4 billion population deepening with a 341 million middle class, meanwhile canny digitally Gen Z shoppers add an all-encompassing 30% annual jump to e-commerce and payments penetration, far ahead of the world. Contrast South Africa's fight with stasis and joblessness even with comparable middle-income demographics. U.S. contenders should champion India first among the BRICS for its sheer consumption surge across retail, fintech and software services.

The average age of the population in Southeast Asian economies is fairly young compared to other regions, therefore, these regions seek to be more receptive to technology, providing U.S. Firms with an opportunity to use this population as fertile ground. The Southeast Asian economies of The Philippines, Vietnam and Indonesia have already demonstrated rapid adoption of mobile wallets and are therefore ideal locations for initial Fintech implementations. Their combined resident population of 190 Million Gen Y and Z-born digital natives were once novelties and now represent the usage behaviors of tomorrow's market-wielding banking, shopping and leisure spending online effectively making Southeast Asia the next multi-billion consumer digital marketplace.

Assessing potential markets involves considering various factors such as market size, growth rate, economic indicators, industry trends, ease of doing business and cultural considerations. A thorough analysis of these factors brings clarity on growth opportunities to make expansion decisions.

The move involves assessing markets by utilizing economic indicators and the potential for expansion. An example: an SMB that focuses on renewable energy may look at India, where government initiatives and surging demand for energy can create real pathways to growth. But sources say the company must weigh obstacles including regulatory shifts and competitive practices from indigenous firms.

Select Key Products or Services as Market Entry Vehicles

When entering new regions, the appropriate product or service to introduce should match the specific drivers of local demand and the specific gaps in the market. Instead of stretching the company's existing bestselling products from home, the objective is to identify adjacency growth opportunities most suitable to serve this market.

For example, a U.S. designer children's clothing brand might find premium pricing restrictions prevent it from generating sales. But the company could conceivably create a value-based line tailored to mid-market parents under a separate brand. This commercial vehicle diverges from flagship offerings but leverages expertise in apparel. Likewise, a U.S. big data analytics provider would net bigger early wins by selling simpler business intelligence tools to SMEs instead of heavy enterprise solutions to conglomerates.

Green energy solutions are promising across regions from Asia to Latin America as are EV vehicles to densification of mobility infrastructure of many congested and polluted megacities with persistent grid failures and fossil fuel shortages. The main business opportunities exist in areas of consumer healthcare that can be translated to India through inexpensive medical devices, telehealth platforms, and remote diagnostics tools given strained public healthcare and insurance limitations. Such expertise resonates with the strengths of American health-tech startups targeting global launchpads.

After identifying a group of potential markets, the next step requires selecting the best products or services for each of these markets. market demand, competitor environment, product/service match, value proposition, and profitability potential. Keeping the above-mentioned aspects in mind will increase the possibilities of success and profitability.

Matching the taste of the target consumer segment is very critical for the success of a product or service. For example, a health technology firm in the U.S. may want to roll out telemedicine services in Southeast Asia in light of the growing Internet presence in the region and demand for healthcare solutions that are conveniently accessible to all. The move, though, needs to be supported with in-depth market research to understand the local need and demand patterns and arouse a product the clients will find useful and willing to pay for.

Justify Value Propositions

Essential to achieving the right product/service mix for market entry is testing the localized value propositions for the target customer segments. Unless the solution gives locals a very good reason to buy it instead of competing options, adoption will be slow. Proof of relevance is usually best established via product trials, customer surveys, and pricing sweet spot identification.

An AI app from a Bay Area startup that seeks to digitize hospital administration work, for example, must first tackle cultural habits. Doctors in most places still prefer human help in booking appointments or maintaining patient logs even if bots are defter. The app needs to show that it supports a hybrid system that mixes automation with human helpers. Pricing also needs to be adjusted to local levels of infrastructure spending rather than U.S. healthcare costs.

Differentiation is important and a clear value proposition is an essential factor in it. For example, the U.S. small and medium-sized business (SMB) in the food industry that is expanding into the European market with organic, non-GMO products. In that case, the U.S. firm's value proposition can highlight health and environmental sustainability, capturing the growing European consumer base that currently weighs these factors in their purchasing decisions.

To justify effectively their value propositions, companies need to emphasize unique features and capabilities, show tangible benefits, provide local references, and adapt messaging to local needs. Then it creates credibility and conveys unique value to customers.

Gain Approvals from Corporate HQ

To gain top-level approval and support from the home office, a persuasive case for market entry must be built on an astute analysis of information. In addition to hard evidence of market attractiveness – such as projections of consumer spending, start-up communities, technology platforms, or policy incentives – softer metrics must indicate cultural compatibility.

Brand sentiment matters. So does understanding the local networks of trade partners and looking for early adopters who signal that this disruption is something real. To convince decision-makers, geography teams organized by regional experts must interpret these signals in context. They need to show why this disruption is truly different and not just another fad. Sophisticated data visualization helps leaders appreciate the subtleties of their risk-reward trade-offs.

Obtaining the green light from headquarters is crucial for resource allocation and strategic alignment. Let's say a software company wants to enter the market in Africa. They'd have to explain in detail why and how they're going to do it, who the target market is, how many customers they expect to attract, what the earnings projections look like, and a plan to overcome local obstacles. This way, they'll get the support and the resources they need.

To obtain agreement from the company head office, firms need a well-stated market opportunity, a convincing financial case, an appraisal of the risks as well as remedies to them, a demonstration of pertinent skills and potentials, and the search for local input/support. By doing these steps, you enhance the chances of getting the project approved.

Top Management's Determination to Win

In addition to reasonable assessments, mindset and motivational focus among upper management greatly influence success abroad. Global ventures require both patience and self-assuredness to push through unforeseen obstacles. If cautious executives greenlight overseas initiatives matter-of-factly, that hesitation trickles down, crippling morale. Similarly, dedication gaps sentence initiatives to die/flutter as soon as adversity briefly surfaces.

The leader's vision must prioritize seizing attractive opportunities abroad of vital importance to buffering against future home-market stagnation. Such determination in turn incentivizes divisions to regard new geographies not as dangerous risks but as indispensable routes to revenue scale, capability refinement, and first-mover spoils. From a brand-voice standpoint, any managerial communication about global learning should stress that improved competitiveness everywhere relies on studying everywhere. Plowing ahead rather than shunning challenges characterizes the more fruitful engagements.

For U.S. SMBs and startups to succeed in emerging markets, it's all about leadership, leadership, leadership. The company's top management must be committed to winning. They must fully endorse the market entry strategy, be willing to adapt to local market conditions, and have the tenacity to rise above obstacles.

Clear goals should be set, vision/strategy communicated, local teams empowered, successes celebrated/setbacks learned from, and contingency plans developed, by top management. Teams are inspired by strong leadership, clear communication, and a commitment to learning/adaption to succeed despite unpredictable emerging market dynamics.

Intelligent emerging market selection demands a thorough examination of growth projections, infrastructure ratings, customer preference mappings, regulatory boosters, and cultural gauges. Segment entry should offer superior unsatisfied solutions to customer pain points versus competition while offering some trials to validate price alignment. For HQ the determination to win and flexible management in the local market are important to start and adjust the international programs. Critical, though, is the firm's leadership amply convinced that the globalization imperative custom fits its future - because the distances and obstacles are easily discouraging.

CHAPTER 5: LOCALIZATION WITH STANDARDIZATION

Globalization has linked worldwide markets, but all local markets still have distinct slants and demands. When SMBs and startups enter emerging markets, they must deftly span the chasm between efficiency-minded standardization and purposeful localization to meet local needs. This chapter outlines some key pointers for intentional localization.

Hire a Genuine Local Market Expert as a Team Leader

Being bilingual is very important for entering and growing a market. John Tan was appointed as Hail's CEO in China because he was influential, connected, and had "guanxi," an important resource for China's business expansion. Tan was a former official in the Ministry of Macro Environment Protection. Tan used to be the main player in obtaining regulatory entries for Hail in China, and he had incredible connections in the government. Tan was also connected to the business network for Hail.

The preferred candidate for a local market expert should have at least ten years of experience successfully starting and scaling ventures in the target market through business upturns and downturns. Look for candidates fluent in the native language of the target location with advanced degrees from top universities in the target country to demonstrate deep expertise. Comprehensive background checks are essential for validating credentials and reputation.

Allow this leader, who drives localization efforts and oversees government relations, to have the authority to make quick decisions in the marketplaces without requiring lengthy approval processes. At the same time, establish an open and transparent two-way conversation to secure agreement on overall direction. Use this leader as a conduit to ensure global alignment when interpreting the home office for the local team.

Quantify Localization Costs and Returns

On properties such as product features, branding, packaging, messaging, alliances, and consumer service, conduct detailed studies of anticipated return against incremental investment needed to localize. Create fiscal models using assumptions sensitivity analyses to model payback, which vary from conservative – i.e., 24 months – to aggressive, for example, six months.

Retrieve quantitative data using concentration-group studies and conjoint analysis. Gather qualitative insights from observation in social listening tools and local bulletin boards. Analyze to determine market size and prioritize potential areas for localization with estimated sales lift and margin upside over cost.

Implement an executive steering committee to govern localization decisions while balancing benefits versus risks, i.e., brand dilution and complexity. Indicate allowable deviations by region while maintaining global brand identity and positioning homogeneity. Continually assess localization programs, cutting those that are not obviously payback-worthy.

Globalized Sales Pitches with Localized Flavors

Ensure that sales materials consistently reflect the global brand promise and value proposition. The peripheral elements such as formats, imagery, and case studies should be localized to match local preferences. The core messaging should be consistent worldwide. Use the global credentials to lead, and provide local market-relevant benefits based on the priority decision drivers.

Make sure that the localization reflects insights from local focus groups, not assumptions or stereotypes. Pay attention to idiomatic language and cultural nuances in the translation process. D-Cloud, a leading IT vendor, increased conversions by 20% with localized webpages featuring local photos and testimonials.

Evaluate the pricing models and discounts' adaptation very carefully to make sure they fit the global strategy. Make sure that the premium positioning matches affordability perceptions in the target market where the product is being sold. Pay attention to the channel conflicts as the localization process increases variance across different regions which should be managed proactively with clear policies.

Understand Local Purchase Decision Drivers

There is wide variation in the relative importance of functional performance, brand prestige, social signaling, and price across countries and segments. Determine the decision drivers and their weights for target segments through ethnographic market research, surveys, and statistical analysis. Weights might be 40% price, 30% prestige, 20% features, and 10% peer adoption. Tailor messaging and positioning accordingly, through localization.

A top-tier global brand must balance a constant burning desire for prestigious global branding with the expectation of affordable pricing and financing options. Constantly re-test assumptions on purchase decisions through A/B panel testing and conjoint analysis as consumer preferences evolve with rising incomes and greater technology penetration. Experimental offerings can be localized; the brand essence must remain global.

Provide Customer Service Despite Costs

Today's consumers, especially in emerging markets, yearn for better-than-average customer service compared to the typical support model for low-cost purchases. Incorporate high-end service costs into your financial projections; consider deploying chatbots and self-service to maximize human capital.

Thoughtfully establish local customer experience centers to build trust and collect first-hand consumer insights. Pay extra for customer support agents who are native speakers of the local language; properly train those agents in cultural practices so their etiquette is unimpeachable.

Think of customer support as an important point of brand differentiation, a chance to earn loyalty through world-class service quality and deepened engagement. Mine your customer analytics for issues and feedback that can improve your product, and develop new local offerings.

Accentuate Local Relevance in User Experience

Localized user interface elements such as color palettes, iconography, date and time formats, and right-to-left text should conform to local conventions. Defaults should be localized to reduce cognitive load but permit individual customization as markets are often far from monolithic.

Bespoke motion libraries were developed to cater to local tastes around animation, transitions, audio cues, and micro-interactions. Usability studies to identify the sticking points and designer iteration to remove the friction.

Fitness app MindNow for its guided meditation audio instructions tailored the pronouns used, the image and language associations, and even the familial terms used based on the app user's gender, region, age, and other attributes. This intense level of personalization led to an 80% increase in app engagement from their women users.

Stay Apolitical and Legally Compliant

Do not take sides in local political, national, or religious debates – remain neutral. Do not assume that our laws and norms extend in any general way to other countries: things like privacy, speech, property, and trade can be very different from country to country. Keep an eye on legal and regulatory tripwires.

Form an advisory board of influential community leaders who are willing to give guidance, open doors, and resolve any issues that may crop up in the important market. Keep the lines of communication open and cooperate with local business leaders for change to show the officials that you mean business, and business only.

Seek advice from local experts when entering the market and as your business expands due to the fluctuating nature of developing market regulations. There may not be legal counsels we define in certain emerging markets, but there are experts or authorities who know how to keep your business free of legal issues. Offer law-specific awareness training to local leadership every year. Continuously evaluate and conduct anti-corruption tests and risk assessments for each business unit.

Successful execution of progressive localization requires visionary global leadership that is willing to invest financially and engage locally for market insights, guidelines and strategic alignment processes that enable autonomous operation within the parameters, and ongoing dialogue not just central reporting. This commitment leads to true agility, customer centricity, and risk management on a global scale.

CHAPTER 6: ENTER LOCAL MARKETS

Pros and Cons of Local Footprints

Doing business in developing countries brings advantages and challenges for U.S. SMBs and startups, which must be calculated. In-country people and operations can help You. Businesses understand the market, develop contacts, get the name out, and provide a local customer experience. A US software company that opened a modest in-country office in Nigeria with a few key hires saw remarkable market traction and sales growth just due to better customer contacts and insights.

On the other hand, establishing wholly owned foreign subsidiaries or businesses increases costs, complications, executive time, and risks. Real estate, specialist hiring, legal compliance, financial reporting, corporate taxes, data protection, and more can all add up quickly in unfamiliar foreign territories. Finding reliable local partners, protecting intellectual property in weaker legal systems, maintaining strong oversight and control of distant foreign subsidiaries or joint ventures, managing linguistic/cultural barriers, and navigating the EPZ, FTZ, SEZ, and other levers…these are all riskier.

Lacking outside know-how, taking on an ambitious emerging-market venture can be costly and perilous. Rather, SMEs and start-ups could obviously take a crawl, walk, run approach to foreign growth. A modest original investment, such as having an independent sales agent or basic sales office, will affordably test those particular waters before committing to a larger, local presence.

Handle Complex Foreign Regulations

Financial systems, regulations, taxes, tariffs, trade policies, bureaucracy, corruption, maturity of infrastructure, and a host of other structural factors constitute any international market. Without local assistance, American SMBs, which have no experience with—or knowledge of—elaborate international rules, protocols, and perils, may find it daunting, even impossible to navigate them.

Establishing relationships and seeking guidance from experienced local staff or consulting firms is necessary to set up your foreign subsidiary's accounting systems, bank relationships, payment flows, customer and vendor agreements, hiring and HR practices, taxes, and more. Staying compliant and avoiding costly errors protects the company from large fines and fosters goodwill with local government authorities.

It is also essential to allocate specific responsibilities to consistently check legal, tax, trade, and regulatory policy changes in your overseas target countries that may require your operations and activities to be altered. Given the volatility and bureaucratic capriciousness in many developing market governments, what is legal one month may be illegal or prohibitively expensive the next. Stay agile and react fast while staying in compliance with local laws.

Respect Local Businesses and Bureaucratic Customs

In addition to the fundamental compliance with legal and financial requirements, it is essential for American companies to understand and attempt to comply with the local business protocol related to communication, relationship building, negotiations, contracts, client entertainment, human resources and other areas. Respect for – and going along with – the local bureaucratic systems and connections, perceived by the West as inefficient or unreasonable, is crucial. Too much deviation from market-specific cultural norms or just resentment towards authorities it is in touch with can easily destroy corporate connections and local trust needed to function successfully for years within smaller, tight-knit communities of developing markets. Encourage local team members to help international leadership understand and play country-specific business conventions, etiquette, communications tones, or even key local partners.

Entry Models with Less Risk

SMBs can test markets without committing too much at once by using independent sales reps, small sales offices and representing larger local distributors in new developing markets.

Sales reps by market may demonstrate goods, initiate early pipeline contacts, solicit customer feedback and identify bona fide demand before setting local roots. Simple sales offices with few people run local demos and meetings. Representing a larger local vendor leverages their infrastructure and emphasizes product-market fit.

Using these more flexible market entry methods, SMBs may pilot test demand, show demand, learn market dynamics versus the competitive landscape and establish local legitimacy before expanding permanently with local facilities and subsidiaries. Continuing to learn simplifies market exit to minimize losses.

Joint Ventures, Acquisitions, Local Subsidiaries

As confidence, expertise, and sales potential increase from initial local scouting, SMBs might advance to shared risk models like JVs or greater control options like local subsidiaries and acquisitions.

Starting a joint venture (JV) with an appropriate local partner enables firms to cheaply reap the benefits of the partner's distribution relationships, regional infrastructure, industry knowledge, brand recognition, and other advantaged assets while sharing the substantial costs, execution risks, and operational resources to individually build this vital early platform.

On the other hand, to establish and fully own a foreign subsidiary or to acquire a synergistic local business provides the highest degree of control and potential upside in a target foreign market but also incurs all downside risk and upfront investment necessary to establish and execute substantial localized operations. These more involved overseas expansion options make sense when prior testing and initial ramp-up have confirmed significant demand and longer-term market prospects.

CHAPTER 7: RISK DETECTION AND CONTROL

Operating in emerging economies carries higher risks than in developed economies. For small and medium enterprises (SMEs) and startups, these overseas markets must already be armed with comprehensive risk management as a strategic imperative for future expansion. Chapter 8 provides a practical, expanded guide to detecting, correcting, and preventing risks, peculiar to these lucrative but challenging markets.

Risk Detection is the First Job of a Local Leader

The main job of the local team is risk management. Their local networks as part of their on-the-ground insights carry much of the burden. They are continuously monitoring for verbal, behavioral, and policy shifts that can cause operations to fail. The detect phase of risk management is when mitigations are the most efficient.

Whenever the subsequent warning signs emerge, quick inspection is required:

1. Suddenly canceling a large supply order or important partnership agreement with no good explanation
2. Major customers refusing to pay invoices on time by contracted terms.
3. Claims for irregular discounts that stray from pre-defined pricing policies or incentive levels
4. An increase in complaints from customers or a significant decrease in product reviews
5. Bold moves by fierce rivals such as extreme price slashing or mass talent raiding
6. Modifications in regulatory frameworks or the industry's political state at a local level

The team should systematically order each risk event by potential business impact and likelihood of occurrence, to guide how much resource allocation the team will commit to investigation and resolution. Those with high-impact threats should get senior leader attention across legal, finance, product engineering, and analytics functions. In contrast, those low-likelihood old issues may just need documentation without substantive actions.

To feed into prevention policy improvement, comprehensive incident timelines and contributing risk factors should be completely compiled. Moreover, comprehensive incident timelines and contributing risk factors should be compiled as a part of prevention policy improvement. This will help to enable data-driven root cause analyses for systemic risks. The ultimate goal is balanced mitigation as situations develop without overreaction or underreaction.

Resolving Local Conflicts

Even when trying to build relationships with key partners, customers or influencers in emerging markets, conflicts can arise over misunderstandings. The initial local team mindset in these situations is important, as pointing fingers often leads to resentment and a refusal to find a middle ground.

Before responding defensively, they should instead strive to understand the reasons underlying grievances through respectful dialogue. Complaint protocols are profoundly divergent in various cultural settings, with Asia historically favoring subtler indirect voicing, while Westerners typically indulge in blunt direct criticism. Once the underlying causes are more apparent, therefore, even simple miscommunication caused by linguistic or business etiquette disparities can often yield a mutual understanding. Demonstrating that parties genuinely care about rectifying problems can go a long way in building relationships.

If tensions keep on after efforts to make peace, then respected third-party advisors who come to the problem with no stake and a different way of looking at it, can wade in and help. Dispassionate mediators are trusted and can tell people what's really what. By and large, it's the last step before you try to get a judge to sort things out and runs a risk of making things far worse between the parties. So, unless you want to cut this person out of your life, no judge.

Leveraging Local Networks for Positive PR

Positive public relations are more than just a good way to dampen specific disputes; they also store up invaluable reputational goodwill to help absorb the occasional controversy or misstep inevitable as we wend our way around emerging markets. So local leadership should actively cultivate and nurture trusted media relationships and visible community influencer ties that will ensure the company's perspective is reasonably represented when crises occur.

This carefully curated constituency helps correct flatly wrong misimpressions, supply context for complex issues, and assure wider stakeholders of the company's steadfastness in maintaining win-win partnerships. Public support from the likes of highly regarded local officials also goes a long way toward pressuring the disputants to explore remedies outside the formal legal channels.

Prime candidates for inclusion in this network: reporters from top local business and industry publications; think tank researchers who disseminate the opinions of policymakers; prominent university academics; and, perhaps most powerfully, high-traffic local bloggers and journalists. Stray afield of these media insiders, and one risks tipping the balance in unpredictable and potentially unsettling directions, sparking second-guessing that no senior executive needs.

Getting Help From Local Government Officials

Since governments have a noteworthy, visible impact on the overall efforts in the subsequent markets, getting the blessing from key local government officials offers significant life insurance. With their insiders' understanding of the process, officials can specify small shifts in the underlying forces pushing policies and corporate teams. They could also quietly mediate feuds or turn on the heat through back channels, unseen by the public.

The local leadership team must take the initiative to forge personal relationships with commerce ministers, party secretaries, regulatory agency heads, and other key officials through regular private meetings where they update officials on local operating investments, new projects, job creation, and community contributions. Any symbolic gestures that can be made such as sponsoring high-profile government conferences, making political campaign donations within legally mandated limits, or sunnily noting officials' policies that prioritize economic growth also accumulate precious goodwill.

The reserve, which is carefully built by positive contributions, is useful in a variety of ways: urging officials to publicly back the company in the face of false accusations of wrongdoing; leaning on bad actors trying to corrupt operations through illicit tactics such as patent infringement; incentivizing officials pushed by growth targets to settle problems quickly and quietly; and creating a long history of win-win local partnerships that can provide support in the face of bad PR.

Distinguish Complaints, Conflicts and Attacks

Not all grievances that surface are genuinely deserving of substantial replies that involve resource mobilizations. The local team must assess the real severity of the issues and adjust any responses in line with that scale before investing effort.

Typical complaints: There will always be certain delays or disruptions in service— a few late orders, the occasional glitchy software release, or some crummy customer service interactions. It's best to deal with these "kitchen table" issues in a prosaic, straightforward way: an apology, a service credit, and a quick resolution for the people directly affected. These common complaints tend to stay in the same hands where they started.

For conflicts that are driven by a carrot or cultural misunderstandings, the company should also diligently examine its potential internal deficiencies before blaming external factors. Common scenarios are over-enthusiastic salesmen taking orders the company can't deliver, misaligned employee incentive structures driving unintended negative behaviors or just plain business process waste in need of systemic improvement. Seeking mediation before getting the company's own house in order is dangerous as all compromise solutions require self-correction commitments.

Serious malicious OFFENSES like intellectual property theft, persistent defamatory propaganda waged against the company across social media or rumors spread throughout town about employees, or severe vandalism designed carefully to damage the company's trade can be signs that anything from unethical competitors to criminal extortion syndicates is coordinating and carrying out assaults against you, according to former consulate official in Monterey, Mexico, for that country's Foreign Ministry. Firms should not obtain or exercise armed forces and personnel, act instead via local legal channels and leverage government and community allies to effectively and proportionally hit back at the culprits. Opposed to conflicts with altruistic origins, not caving into shenanigans would act as a deterrent against future such incidents.

Risks from Supply Chains

Supply chains see rising disruptions from economic fluctuations, cyber threats, climate change, etc. Possibilities rise all around from profound changes in the global eco-political landscape, financial systems, and country/regional power disequilibria. U.S. firms, small or big, need to adopt strategies resilient to:

To reduce risks concentrated in any one area, utilize suppliers and production facilities across different geographic areas. Having alternate suppliers and facilities situated in various countries provides continuity if a particular area experiences disruption.

Boost the amount of inventory and take the possibility of transport or border congestion into account. Enhancing security inventory levels. While boosting stock can be costly, it also secures a safeguard for unforeseen delays.

Incorporate next-generation technologies such as AI, blockchain, and IoT (Internet of Things) sensors to enhance traceability and agility across the supply chain. These tools enable instantaneous visibility of inventory and shipments, making it easier to spot bottlenecks.

Create contingency plans and risk mitigation strategies by identifying alternative suppliers and modes of transportation in advance. Furthermore, training employees from various locations equips them with fluency in transferring work from one location to another when site-specific disruptions take place.

Give priority to the resilience of the supply chain and its stability over merely minimizing costs and lean-time efficiencies. Some slack and redundancy and excess capacity allow organizations to better handle disruptions. We need to think much more about resilience than return on the bottom line in some sense.

Create a complete set of guidelines for crisis management, such as identifying substitute vendors and ensuring that the supply chain is flexible.

Hold frequent exercises and perfect response strategies in order to heighten readiness for supply chain disturbances. Nurture reciprocal information lounging with different territories to institute a global supply chain tribulations retort grid.

As global disruptions become both more frequent and massive, having a stable supply chain is becoming a characteristic that sets your company apart from the competition. Being proactive in developing resilience strategies will be the key to thriving companies that navigate the challenges around the corner for those still struggling operationally with continuity disruptions and natural events.

Legal Compliance

As regulations continue to evolve in various emerging-market geographies, investing in ongoing localized training enables on-the-ground teams to maintain compliance with employment guidelines, financial reporting requirements, environmental regulations, data privacy standards, and anti-corruption laws. Absent vigilant internal legal and compliance acumen attuned to emerging developments, organizational oversight vulnerabilities leave doors open over time to potentially crippling fines, arrest threats, or reputation-clamoring violations inviting further adversarial attacks.

Policies, operating procedures, and staff training programs should be reviewed no less than every quarter as regulations change. Local laws often contradict or exceed U.S. practices, and therefore require thoughtful localized reconciliations and market-specific guidance. Maintaining a high-quality law firm retainer injects forward-leaning insight when regulatory change is announced. Retaining credibility through guidelines honed in adherence provides essential leverage when business conflicts arise with partners, customers, or special-interest groups.

Unbiased Reporting Channels from Market Frontlines

It is very likely for leaders at the headquarters to be unable to recognize distortions in reporting by local emerging market teams who excessively care about being blamed for missing performance targets and tell only good news. They are also encouraged to downplay brewing problems to protect regional growth prospects. Consequently, creating a confidential independent reporting system to allow frontline staff and partners to anonymously submit risk alerts with no fear of retribution is the perfect proactive solution.

By going through a different channel and without going through their direct superiors, managers and employees remove huge impediments to providing candid local insight on business issues or early warning signals. Automating sensor data on inventory levels, vehicle movements, technology infrastructure performance, and equipment operation also gives unfiltered insight into problems that need to be investigated and mitigated. Relying on humans who report to controlled hierarchies creates analytic blind spots.

All Critical Documents Are Required to be in Bilingual Versions

Years later, when a business relationship falls apart in a foreign market, contracts, joint venture agreements and compliance policies drafted only in English or in a localized language, but without a corresponding English version, can cause huge misunderstandings. Disputes overseas can be enough of a headache without the added trouble of incompatible interpretations of key passages. At that point, it is all but impossible to defuse tensions and resolve fights that no one had anticipated back when life was a bowl of cherries. Without legal terms exactly matching English-language equivalents, companies are doubly blind.

It is therefore a critical risk mitigation strategy to require bilingual documents on all material terms down to the fine print in alliances, vendor arrangements, and government contracts. In the long run, it also pays by eliminating linguistic ambiguity around privacy safeguards, patent rights exports and import controls, product performance claims, and much more.

While it can be three times as expensive to carefully translate every article pre-landing under legal expert supervision, the insurance policy translates into a concrete decrease in linguistic leaks whenever the predictable falling out of foreign-market relations does detonate its claims and threats. Thus, it is advisable for a small- to medium-sized firm with the funds to a wise idea to enter the tougher emerging markets due to their more potential growth and profits. It is all about team quality, regulation rigor and ally connections with the ability to handle crises first. Back the team alone equates to effective operate-through art. Once the procedures are in place, you are focused on growing, rather than dealing endlessly with attacks.

CHAPTER 8: SELLING WITH LOCAL FLAVORS

Leveraging, But Not Relying on, US Brand Power

U.S. technology brands entering emerging markets often initially rely heavily on perceived notions of superior American innovation and quality. However, as local competition intensifies, merely projecting an elite foreign brand image eventually leads to lost sales to more affordable or culturally aligned competitors.

SMBs and startups must strategically leverage their U.S. brand equity to open doors but then rapidly demonstrate tangible value-add through localization, partnerships, pricing, and customer intimacy that resonates with the needs of targeted customer segments.

For example, advanced analytics software from a U.S. firm may enjoy a brief honeymoon phase from early adopters impressed by Silicon Valley pedigree. However mainstream adoption is unlikely to gain traction without local language interfaces, integrations with popular local e-commerce platforms, pricing tiers for budget-conscious SMBs, and the ability to customize algorithms incorporating local data sets.

The key is to ride the coattails of U.S. brand reputation to attract initial customers but not depend complacently on such 'halo effect' goodwill to drive growth. Brand building should project premium technology leadership as manifest through locally impactful applications purpose-built for emerging market opportunities.

Identify Optimal Marketing Channel

Emerging digital marketing landscapes with platform uniqueness and fragmentation require U.S. SMBs to conduct extensive due diligence instead of assuming Facebook or Google search dominance mirroring Western markets. Local platforms like Baidu in China or niche social apps like ShareChat in India command significant market share in online discovery.

SMBs should partner with digital marketing agencies deeply rooted in the local terrain that can map out profiles of current and emerging channels vis-a-vis target user demographics, geo-linguistic behavior, purchasing power, and intent signals. Granular analysis is imperative to correctly judge reach, and ROI potential and optimize ad formats and budgets across platforms. No single channel delivers the majority of traction.

For example, premium real estate targeted to the Indian diaspora may find traction across traditional property portals like MagicBricks as well as custom influencer campaigns on ShareChat. High-touch sales support seals deals. However, assumptions based simply on Western platforms risk suboptimal customer targeting, messaging, and conversions.

Utilize Messaging Locals Like, not HQ Prefer

U.S. SMBs must tune messaging to align with cultural nuances around visual aesthetics, celebratory occasions, family values, and metaphorical language considered engaging in the region. Rather than forced word translations, work with local subject matter experts and translators to first identify intrinsic human motivations associated with the product- promises of status enhancement, community belonging, nurturing support, etc.

Then develop locally resonant brand stories and experience narratives layered around the product promise conveyed through relevant cultural memes. Finally produce localized creative assets across various formats optimized not just for semantic meaning but contextual emotional appeal based on psychographic insights.

Regular customer research, focus grouping, and user testing of results are key to iterating toward messaging mastery. Periodic checks against global branding guidelines maintain the integrity of brand identity while crucially flexing for local relevance.

Emphasize Sales over Management

The early market development emphasis should be less on building out extensive organizational processes and hierarchies and more on empowering a nimble field sales team to hustle for traction in relatively untested waters. Sales leadership skills ought to exhibit as much raw streetwise deal-making creativity as textbook selling fundamentals when novel products first encounter opaque red tape.

The founding sales team carries huge execution risk but also forms the proving bed from which to precipitate future scale. Their leadership archetype to admire may exhibit traits akin to determined athletic coaching rather than risk-averse corporate stewardship. Employee appraisals would evaluate urgent KPIs like monthly active customer acquisition over backend efficiency metrics which can be subsequently streamlined later.

Cooperate with Local Stars and Influencers

Rather than Hollywood or Instagram celebrities seen as out-of-touch with local realities, consumers better relate to homegrown cinema personalities, sports heroes, pop artists, or youth icons organically positioned to seed and validate consumption trends in areas like diet preferences, fashion statements, or smartphone deals via their mass appeal.

SMB sponsorships and partnerships can promise exclusive product trial access to these influencers as social media fodder for authentic storytelling. Leveraging backstage drama or heroic protagonist narratives fused visually with branded engagements can captivate the precise psychographic niches across regions within large but fragmented countries.

Get Approval and Support of Local Authorities

Instead of being intimidated by perceptions of opaque bureaucratic red tape or paper-pushing regulators, U.S. SMBs should proactively court interest and endorsement from municipal chambers of commerce, economic zone administrators, and industry trade group executives through programs that promise to uplift their communities.

Patient explanations on how cutting-edge pilot initiatives could elevate constituencies with jobs, infrastructure, or skilling can organically turn influential gatekeepers into partners. However, the instinct to casually attempt bribery must be avoided utterly. Trusted project advisors with nuanced policy insights help correctly navigate federalism dynamics between central approvals and regional leaders' growth agendas.

Innovative Customers Services

Emerging economy consumers who are wary of unreliable product quality normally crave quick service support but the US companies worry about the costs of providing the customer services. The impasse demands creative hybrid models.

Self-service chatbots deftly triage cases by complexity before human hand-offs. Remote video troubleshooting guides users through basic repairs before dispatching spare parts or technicians. Cloud analytics predicts high failure risk equipment for proactive preventive maintenance.

Secondary authorized reseller partnerships share real-time inventory visibility enabling speedy sourcing and traceability. Empowered online communities provide peer-based product support and feature enhancement ideas. Such mechanisms blending digital tools with a human touch deliver localized support within infrastructure constraints for global-grade reliability.

Build Influencer Ecosystems

In emerging markets where traditional advertising may have partial reach and credibility, building organic influencer and microcelebrity ecosystems can offer alternative traction channels by seeding positive word-of-mouth through creative storytelling crafted for different niches.

Instead of impersonal paid sponsorships, collaborating to develop exclusive product co-creation opportunities allows influencers to integrate brands meaningfully into autobiographical narratives shared as first-person testimonials carrying credibility. "Superfans" among followers amplify messages across their networks kicking off viral social cascades. Hashtag activism sustains momentum.

Technology tools can today map cross-platform topologies of followers and influencers selling competing or complementary offerings. Such insights help discover untapped pockets of opportunity audiences and optimize messaging interventions sequentially for sustained impact with analytics measuring every step.

Structure Fair Incentives for Channel Partners

While direct sales may seem the only way to control the customer experience, building partnerships with local distributors, retailers, and brokers leveraging their physical capillarity and customer trust facilitates rapid physical reach unviable through owned infrastructure, especially for SMBs.

Incentives should encourage win-win partnerships for partners through margins and channel loyalty programs allowing co-creation of differentiated value propositions like bundled offerings, tie-ins with financial services, innovative promotions, etc beyond plain reselling. Clear communication, simplified processes, and marketing resources support boost motivation and channel health.

Localize Pricing Models

Purchasing power variations mean emerging markets require purposeful pricing models reflecting affordability constraints of even quality-conscious customer segments beyond only premium targeting. SMBs must localize pricing architecture balancing the ability to pay against the total cost of delivery incorporating operational realities.

Tactics may span stripped-down "lite" versions, usage or outcome-based models, pooled subscription licensing to maximize sharing, credit integration with local fintech players, auctions or reverse bidding formats, and closing "gateway deals" attracting anchors to de-risk future expansion.

Continuous optimization responding to demand elasticity and competitive dynamics drives growth.

Partnering with Local Innovation Hubs

Emerging hubs like China's Shenzhen or India's Bangalore home clusters of agile product innovators who can rapidly iterate electronics, software, and mechanical modules tailored for local needs from factory automation gadgets to mobile gaming accessories.

Partnering via flexible development contracts, hackathons, or technology license agreements allows U.S. SMBs to leverage such indigenous innovation capabilities for localized product extensions while providing these hubs exposure to American expertise in areas like sensors, analytics, or new materials through open API ecosystems and feeds of Silicon Valley trends.

Optimizing Talent Management

Attracting and retaining top talent in emerging markets demands localized talent branding on platforms Gen Z frequents, showcasing cutting-edge product problems that motivate, and respect regional variance in expectations on work-life balance, empathy, and purpose.

Optimize processes leveraging online collaboration tools balancing business formalities with Startup cultures where creative freedom, lack of excessive hierarchy, and healthy camaraderie keep teams engaged. Allow horizontal mobility across functions and geographies for multifaceted exposure removing barriers to learning. Share the inspirational vision and welcome candid bottom-up feedback.

Demand Ethics while Respect Local Customs

Despite local customs involving gift-giving, establishing no-exception processes that enforce ethical boundaries across activities like sales kickbacks, procurement bias, and HR wrong-doings prevents "slippery slopes". Training should clearly distinguish between cultural norms, personal favors, and unethical actions. Framework contracts transparently log partner interests. Strong whistleblower policies enable confidential reporting.

Tone from the top backed by financial controls, audits incorporating ethics metrics into performance management, and open town halls for anonymous queries reinforce integrity culture as central to long-term success rather than merely regulatory compliance.

Agility Is Crucial

Emerging markets demand quick launch speeds for products, promotions, and partnerships given dynamic shifts in consumer preferences, competitive moves, and policy changes. U.S. SMBs can embrace technologies like cloud infrastructure, APIs, analytics, and social listening tools to compress time-to-impact for localization, boost decision velocity, and coordinate regional responses.

APIs enable rapid integration with local fintech tools and e-commerce marketplaces to accelerate digital channel adoption. Sentiment analysis identifies brand challenges in real time. Collaboration apps assist global-local coordination. Stack modularization helps reconfigure offerings faster. Digital as centerstage delivers sales agility.

CHAPTER 9: REWARDING PARTNERSHIPS

Seek Matching Partners

When US small and medium-sized businesses first enter unfamiliar markets in the developing world, they should consider partnering with local companies to reduce political and currency risks-- a no-brainer. They may also be able to learn the terrain and get their products to market faster by leveraging local strengths in new product or business development, sourcing, channel management, and other capabilities. For example, many local business people possess an intuitive understanding of the differences between the tastes and needs of consumers in different cities in China, a country with some 2,600 distinct cities that US business people will take many, many years to understand fully, if ever, on their own. Also, the Chinese and Indians alone can offer US firms access to a billion new consumers.

Structure Effective Partnership Models

Adaptability is essential in crafting partnership structures that match the growth phase, levels of uncertainty, and potential advancement of pooled resources. Instead of essentially cloning Western-style contracts, customize protocols to the range of activities, whether they involve one-shot pilots, complete interlocked product-service sets, elaborated marketing alliances, or merger-like external ventures.

But it is equally important to clearly draw the lines of authority, especially over mission-essential matters such as branding, ownership of intellectual property, access to proprietary customer databases, establishment of quality standards, and setting of performance metrics. Phased-in processes govern the introduction of improved routines and the stages of value addition. Devices for conflict resolution head off destabilization of partnerships.

Shared interests are crucial in sustaining collaborations, yet preparedness for eventualities requires built-in durability.

Transfer Capabilities to Local Partners

Arms-length dealings may seem safer for protecting the informational goods that provide an advantage against adversaries in new markets, but strategically transferring capacities to local partners and nurturing trust are the crucial foundations of lasting collaboration. The drawbacks of lost knowledge and the delays of asymmetric dependence are real but manageable. Safeguarding core IP through encryption, or revealing selectively to foreign allies via APIs, is sensible. But sharing non-core skills, savvy about operations, and a worldwide perspective benefits partners and investors alike. Both sides access value-adding assets, and can seek broader, richer opportunities to build mutual upside. The risks of empowering partnerships are outweighed by the chances for shareholder wealth creation unaccompanied by free-riding imitators.

Integrate with Partner's Team in Early-Stage Product Development

Incorporating specific partners into the initial stages of product development, such as early product conceptualization, design reviews, and prototyping, gives them the ability to draw on their knowledge of local customers' needs and the components available on the gray market to improve products. It also helps companies obtain rapid feedback through their distribution networks. This kind of integration differs from just hiring a contract manufacturer after a product's specifications are set in stone. By making use of partners in these early stages, it allows engineers to come up with new designs that are better suited to market realities. It also provides a benefit associated with partners and companies working through the inevitable difficulties that come with producing the first runs of new products. This way, when the heavy work of producing, retailing, and maintaining the product begins, the partnership has already been tested and solidified.

Leverage Partners' Government Relationships

In addition to the main products, partners in developing markets also contribute important accumulated informal knowledge in order to understand the rules, procurement norms, and government relationships necessary to obtain the required approvals. Proactively engage local partners to engage with officials, rather than endure bureaucratic obstacles that destroy value. Recognize that although systematic cronyism may be immoral, every society has legitimate political connections that, once understood, can lead to an ethical win-win situation. Partners can help you align genuinely value-added projects and long-term business success to form loyal relations that do not need to be compromised.

Work with Partners in Go-To-Market Planning

Jointly created entry strategies, which forge close relationships with local market insights, garner more context, wisdom, and buy-in for successful execution compared to strategies developed in isolation. The initiation of consent for marketing assets design, channel packaging, pilot targets, and a multi-phased investment roadmap gains considerably from direct partner engagements rather than delayed handoffs of fully gelled plans. Such lead-user collaborations have drastic implications for cross-functional learning and the resulting product and service innovations.

Particularly, introducing new product categories in emerging markets that are mired in uncertainty calls for a collaborative orientation in planning, deployment, and learning. Partners with substantial "skin in the game" capabilities gain invaluable ground–truth "sensing" and "agile adaptation" that cannot be matched by any corporate army of market researchers or hard-nosed finance professionals.

Build Lasting Win-Win Relationships

Effective collaboration in developing economies is a far more sophisticated affair than a simple opportunistic wealth transfer. Sustainable business relationships in places where trust and contracts are often ineffective necessitate a sincere, shared understanding of the future, one that enables both sides to envision ambitions that could profit both. They must share knowledge motivated by mission—not just profit—be responsive in the face of conflict, and support their allies when times are tough. Such slates need to provide the kind of permanence that allows for the consolidation of various complementary, specialized nodes into something like a scaled strategy. If you think of a very specifically crafted partnership as being like an actual body, then it needs a spine and muscles and lots of inputs to move forward fast or precisely, depending on what's required of it. Those who find it more cost-effective to remain purely tactical are — sooner or later — consigning themselves to the super-efficient, risk-sharing, control-conserving orientation of Discoverers. Only more adroit, agile, and intuitive.

Share Customer Relationships

Instead of just focusing on transactions, trusted collaborations should manage customer relationships together. They can collaborate seamlessly instead of dividing the business by sales territories or channels. This will enable unified customer infrastructure, helpdesk systems, and channels for feedback from end to end after sales. In addition, customers also expect a consistent journey from digital advertising to retail showrooms and after-sales inquiries. Partnership backends will not affect customer trust at any touchpoint. This requires technology integration, resource application, and combined metrics and incentives.

Sunset Unsuccessful Pilots Quickly

The Lean Startup approach assumes that most early-stage experimental partnerships will disappoint expectations despite their potential. Instead of intensifying efforts in difficult test projects, it integrates metrics for graduate evaluation of engagement, capability development, and growth milestones into pilot governance frameworks to assess the true potential of these partnerships. It is important to stop getting involved in expensive relationships that do not benefit either party, despite efforts to make them work. The resources saved can be used in other relationships.

Of course, patience in keeping partnerships during the trial period may reveal long-term benefits. However, abandoning the partnerships that will not withstand the business cycles can save resources and allow focus on scaling the partnerships that really work.

Maintain the Same Deal Governance

As startups grow and become established businesses, it's essential that they establish principles that will maintain a consistent approach to similar deals across the variety of partnerships and channels they are likely to pursue. While the model for initial projects might emphasize adaptability, the need for scaling makes it essential to build an approach that would be used throughout the company. This is particularly important as more people become involved in reviewing and approving arrangements. To the founding team, this can seem less nimble and less improvisational. These playbooks codify the processes that ensure onboarding processes, infrastructure integration, capability building, milestone setting, and decoupling including lessons learned and best practices established during previous deals at your company. At a time when partnership types and stages are proliferating, stable, consistent methods of examining overall progress are essential.

Celebrate Mutual Achievements

Each year, our partnership summits help create an inclusive atmosphere by celebrating the progress we have made together in a relaxed setting without the usual business pressure. By giving out awards, allowing our leaders to talk about their personal experiences and holding informal gatherings, we strive to come closer together and share what makes us who we are. We also take great pride in overcoming challenges as one, and being vulnerable to one another as we hear from more junior members that have helped shape who we are in so many ways. Whether hearing about someone's family, hobbies, volunteer work or taking part in a collaborative activity, we keep each other uplifted during times of uncertainty. We also remember that regardless of what is happening outside of our own group, we have a great sense of purpose and warm camaraderie that will bind us together forever.

Plan-B

Despite forming strong alliances, unexpected problems from changing government policy, developments, or a move by rivals can alter the balance of power swiftly and imperil the trust between allies. To be ready for such shock, defense strategists must calculate various "what-if" scenarios and assess risks regularly. By then having open discussions about possible future limitations, where can capacity be over-taxed? and what sideline markets could become front lines? A deeper understanding of the points where adjustments will be crucial.

Would also signal partners' mutual commitment, who would be reassured about each other when market conditions become shaky. Then both sides could avoid overreaction or underreaction, and fight as one front by defending together when a threat comes.

Limit Dependence Risks

Deep integration with long-standing partners is key to making the most of their complementary expertise. At the same time, relying too heavily on any one partner leaves you vulnerable to the possibility that they could exploit their advantage over you. To guard against this, you should always keep your other options open, and be sure to voice any grievances instead of just walking away. Keep your core relationships strong—maybe no more than two or three for any one function—and that will limit the potential for any one partner to abuse his role. These tighter, more strategic relationships could even encourage more cooperative behavior from your established partners. In other words, cooperation should be the goal, not a bunker mentality.

Mentor Promising Startups

Entering the market successfully establishes the groundwork for becoming an industry leader in the future by guiding and supporting promising start-ups and entrepreneurs. Such individuals may end up changing the way business is done in today's world. The key is to search for these future builders in their midst, reach out to them, and get immersed in their enterprises - especially when the technologies, operation models, and market adoption they aim to bring forth are disruptive even by today's standards.

Gain everything. Gain management time, patient capital, and allies who open doors wide. Expect mentorship in return, a guided journey to shape and conquer the future. Walk the distance with them, help co-create the future together, organize the co-branded customer board summits, and fund and lead their pilots with well-thought-out road mapping.

When mentor-powered start-ups proliferate, they will tip the incumbent hierarchy through decades of marginal innovations. They will also fill up the innovation pipeline by defusing boredom and cynicism - a problem that today's most praised start-ups often overlook, but the problem a power law-distributed innovation ecosystem must face.

Quit Dysfunctional Legacy Relationships

As organizations and ecosystems evolve, some legacy partnerships risk becoming dysfunctional due to Founder disconnects, trust deficits from leadership changes, or complacency from misaligned incentives across functions. Resist the temptation to paper over glaring cracks with transient reconciliations. Summon the courage to kindly unravel partnerships where enduring sources of friction suggest a widening delta in values, priorities, and direction.

Free up stranded resources to invest in new engagements that link energetically to an organization's purposeful growth. Honor where an organization has come from but recognize when paths have irretrievably diverged. Change can be wrenching, but judicious pivots open up auspicious new vistas.

Building ventures with partners is a delicate dance of commitment and flexibility, integration and optionality, confidence building and contingency planning. Get these variables right, following the principles outlined here, so external ecosystems richly multiply rather than hallow out internal capabilities.

CHAPTER 10: FINANCIAL MANAGEMENT

To effectively exploit the lucrative growth potential of emerging markets while adeptly managing unfamiliar risks, U.S. SMBs and startups must possess sophisticated capabilities. This chapter offers a comprehensive playbook covering the following major areas to facilitate the daunting task ahead.

Plan and Manage Capital Professionally

Thorough financial planning starts with comprehensive models accurately evaluating financial forecasts for market entrance localization expenditures, cautious multi-year financial performance plans measured to category standards, and sufficient risk tolerance considerations in response to potential instability. Estimations must adjust for greater promotional expenses due to divisional, antagonistic environments; transport fees due to infrastructural waste; manufacturing personalization; workforce training disbursements to close capabilities chasms; and buffers against constant interruptions.

Ensuring sufficient initial financing creates stability with staged fund allotments linked to watermark prompts rather than a straight disbursement. Minute object-level accountability through an accountable-versus-authenticated fiscal forecast readjusts readily. Cautious top-line assumptions with stretch costs guarantee trim profitability cycles despite headwinds.

To keep prescribed liquidity coverage buffers amidst variable cash collection cycles, need trade finance in the form of credit insurance, bonded warehousing, and installment billing by customer classification anticipated payment capacity mapping. By eschewing flamboyant promotion demonstrates financial legitimacy minimizes appearance dangers entices the cheapest possible capital.

Allocate Adequate Funds for Global Projects

Exploring finance sources beyond normal loans includes angel investing, hands-on private equity, high-growth country-based venture capital, and revenue-based finance in varying stages, each with its own associated risks and returns. For example: specialist venture debt bridges key early milestones creating clear proof points growing Series A equity valuations accelerating scaling expertise as needed. International partnering with patient impact investors provides growth capital and local know-how to drive community trust. They are combining government grants, export subsidies and insured trade finance to address incremental emerging market risks, optimize capital structure, and minimize costs. Selective Stock Exchange listing evaluations fund later regional expansion on better-aligned investor bases and reward early-team employees through that growth. Technology solutions, digitizing latent assets like inventory, invoices, and contracts, unlock new working capital collaterals finally closing cash flow and liquidity gaps. Proactive investor relationship management assures ongoing funding alignment across cycles ensuring forever momentum.

Administer Currency, Taxes, and Profit Repatriation

A coherent and strategically thoughtful risk management strategy on currency is indispensable across translation, transaction, accounting and economic dimensions due to the emerging market volatility. Fit-for-purpose financial instruments need calibration in nuances across currency pairs, exposures, and risk appetites.

Compliance shall assure local regulations and OECD Guidelines coordination among impacted countries and the generation of clear transfer pricing policies. Active but solid repatriation mechanisms include economic substance doctrines, bilateral tax treaties and reinforced regional headquarters vehicles. Timely annual compliance confirmation shall update stakeholders.

The depth of such worries mandates solid auditors and law firms well versed in international tax laws rather than risky shortcuts leading to devastating penalties eating away total returns.

Adopt a Flexible Pricing Structure

Analyzing local income pyramids helps develop dynamic good-better-best price bundling by balancing pricing metrics from the willingness to pay studies against realistic delivered cost structures across the value chain and including R&D expenses to tailor specifications, specialized marketing, dedicated production capacities, distribution reach, and after-sales service investments.

Tactics can include stripped-down "lite" versions that reduce the bill of materials costs while protecting core IP. Or usage or outcome-based models with downside protection, only charging value realized, thus minimizing purchasing barriers. Bundled group licensing can enable creatively pooled affordability.

Co-branded financing partnerships, chosen strategically after careful due diligence, can provide innovative credit integration offers through easy low-interest installment schemes. Anchor tenant subscription programs with marquee clients can provide reference ability that draws wider second-wave adoption.

Prevent Financial Missteps

Thoughtlessly assuming extravagant travel spending or shady "facilitation payments" to intermediaries frequently risks charges of implied corruption dramatically increasing backfilled costs not considered during budgeting. Another pitfall is assuming slick marketing automatically translates into sales without addressing product-market fit, pricing mismatches, or ecosystem alliances. Trying to defend entry barriers or cultural knowledge deficiencies instead of proactively offsetting capability deficiencies through reputable third-party partners sustains predictable decay curves alarmingly emblematic across flops.

Embracing transparency as an elixir for myths enables uncovering positive black swans through grass-roots participatory dialogue with customers, collaborators, and regulators.

Structure Foreign Exchange Benefits

A number of principles govern the writing of Export contracts that will allow a company to systematically recover upside from directional emerging market currency trends. One is to create a mechanism that allows the company to strategically time the receipt of payment from its customer base so that hard currency is paid to the company when the local currency is strong. A second principle is to ensure that the company is not obligated to pay its suppliers in hard currency until after most of its obligation to its customers has been satisfied. In other words, the company creates a natural hedge through the timing of its contractual obligations, in a sense keeping faith with the local currency without the use of derivatives. This timing issue will be introduced in more detail when we discuss the actual structure of the Export Contract a little after this section.

Timely Payment Terms

With firm and insistent resolve, sellers should demand concrete and punctual payments, milestone tracking, and legal assurance of concluded obligations while sometimes striving to extend understanding by allowing some room for maneuvering on strategic partnerships to necessitate cannibalizing inceptive nurturing.

Give and take, like accommodating the client's temporary hold-back for legitimate causes, should earn time but unperturbed tardiness or independent desire for deeper compromise warrant immediate no-alikes of penalties, lawsuits, or even consignment halt for sellers who prefer deterrence to dopey suppliers.

Bank with Global Transferability

While local working capital financing suits recurrent operations, strategic growth priorities necessitating flexible US dollar funding for convertibility suitability demand global banking partners providing convenient repatriation channels, diversified cross-border trade financing and customized risk-sharing solutions enabling aggressive geographical expansions beyond domestic banking constraints.

As emerging markets further integrate with global financial infrastructure, regulation, digital standards and incentives deliberately designed to facilitate its renaissance are designed to be banked on by international banks that can't fund this transformation alone.

Upgraded trade, credit and forex solutions structure the investment and execution risks that once served as a practical limit to global integration: now, it is at the core of emerging market connectivity.

Financial discipline, risk management, regulation and global connectivity underpin each of these core areas, growing collectively on the strength of business practices pioneered by aggressive growth US SMBs and startups with the ambition and appetite to develop functional capabilities out of comparative history, extending into the future. Ongoing successful commercial commitments always begin with first meeting the technical needs of each model.

CHAPTER 11: SUSTAIN COMPETITIVENESS

US Products or Services Maybe Outdated Too

It is important to note that the products and services offered by United States (US) companies may not be as up-to-date or competitive in emerging markets. Consumers do not just accept whatever American companies sell. US businesses must compare the top 3 selling US items by major category with the most recent competitive alternatives. Comparisons by parameter (market share trends, consumer sentiment, feature sets, real-world performance, ecosystem interoperability, pricing, channel incentives) comprise a US competitiveness scorecard.

Declining scores necessitate investments to fill in missing functional capabilities through local partnerships, component substitutes, or internal development. Failure to routinely re-evaluate against advancing indigenous innovation risks erosion of brand equity from outdated claims of superiority.

Develop New Solutions Tailored to New Markets

In addition to adapting our existing portfolio, we tailor innovative solutions for high-potential emerging markets to fuel growth. Our embedded design teams immerse themselves in customers' lives to uncover challenges and constraints that become opportunities for radical rethinking. Unreliable electricity, for example, pushes medical device makers to minimize battery use or switch to renewables.

Cross-functionally designed workshops with local partners reset boundaries as stimulation for globally scalable ideas that survive tougher tests. What seems like crazy high-risk concepts get concentrated business case development to demonstrate commercial viability and warrant internal investment.

Monitor New Competitors

As barriers disappear worldwide, keeping an eye on the playing field at all times is critical. Attuned sales partners will report suspicious activity changes that signal the formation of new corporate subsidiaries, divisions or start-up entrants heading for untended niches. Network analysis, domain registration monitoring, targeted talent poaching outreach and stealth site reverse image searches can help confirm threats. First-mover partnerships, investments or selective M&A can quickly shore up capability gaps that threaten to turn into long-term relationships that demand that they either stretch their capabilities dangerously or walk away. Annual strategy simulations fed with competitive intelligence inputs allow the stress-testing of initiatives for resilience.

Driving Values Up Through Local R&D

R&D success in a locale goes well beyond patents. It is evident in leading research influence, notable sales contribution, significant cost savings, and a brand lift. Centers mature into regional hubs where decorated papers are published, major open-source IP is contributed, and university technical programs are spearheaded.

Despite initially adapting existing offerings, R&D centers architected for local ecosystem immersion enable Made-for-Market breakthroughs. This kind of localized innovation can result in disruptive and responsible creations like affordable vehicle lines for emerging nations. Picture a Silicon Valley garage with its most impressive attributes but located in growth market domains.

Seek Collaborations with Local Startups

Screening frameworks move beyond assessing business viability to unpack start-up motivations and synergies. Assessments weigh readiness for industry credentials, IP protection, relocation, portfolio alignment and most importantly commercialization capacity. Relationships build from the proof points of capabilities through contracted pilots, minority investments and climaxing in rigorous acquire mechanics. Investing in high-potential people. Win-wins hinge on clear value propositions with shared priorities -- not evaporating at the first hump, storm, or even whether after quick payouts happen.

Local Innovations Provide Opportunities Too

A core analytics capability organizes fragmented qualitative market reports and quantifies engineering customer deployments. Behavioral pattern detection algorithms and predictive models link disconnected data into strategic foresight and emerging use cases.

Key insights establish C-suite backing for global R&D influence aligned to regional investment priorities. International centers of excellence speed testing and transfer of niche innovations of wider application. Two-way innovation gateways circulate knowledge.

Embrace Local Culture and Customs

Building trust and loyalty with partners, authorities, and consumers means respecting their cultural traditions and values. This involves adopting proper etiquette, recognizing holidays, avoiding thoughtless blunders, celebrating heritage diversity, and actively backing community causes.

Progressive policies support inclusive, ethical work cultures that make local teams feel genuinely valued as crucial knowledge conduits. Sensitivities change by territory, requiring constant checkups of attributes. It is difficult. The sensitivities investment's return on investment is there.

Stay Ahead of Regulatory Changes

Entities that are heavily dependent on import/export and/or those that are sub-scale may face a disproportionate risk of disruption from the sudden imposition of new non-tariff barriers, through major revisions to product standards, or by new caps on foreign ownership. The establishment of central and/or regional response teams can provide expertise in multiple disciplines necessary to assess compliance gaps and evaluate restructuring options and contingency plans.

Ongoing monitoring tools include government notifications, relevant industry forums, legal digests, and key revisions to WTO reporting. Periodic simulation models can be used to test strategic agility under stress. Connectivity to government regulators and trade policymakers may provide previews of future actions or highlight areas of continuous improvement during transitions.

Prepare for Local Infrastructure Challenges

Volatility of power, congested transportation routes, and other infrastructure choke points make operational reliability a challenge. Lobbying officials for upgrades is a necessary but slow process, so in the interim, we get creative. Blanketing our bases we have alternative supply chains, multimodal transportation, off-the-grid connectivity/generation, and buffer inventories.

Team IDs infrastructure projects with our trade associations so instead of "us vs. the world," it is a "collaborative approach" benefitting all. Solar plants, bonded warehouses, and digital customs upgrades do not just help us, they help the community and make your operations more efficient, too. So, necessity breeds resourcefulness and resilience.

Protect Intellectual Property Rights

Enforcement of IP safeguards remains inconsistent across jurisdictions despite recent advances. A comprehensive security program requires coordinated efforts in trademarks, patents, and industrial design registration locally and internationally. It relies on constant watch and swift counter-claims, and awareness campaigns for partners and employees by emphasizing the importance of protection.

Public-private cooperation is credited with raising IPR standards through such measures as exchanges of inspectors, judicial training programs, and working to establish a broad framework for harmonization. Counterfeiters are defeated by strong deterrence. No ethical standard supports willful appropriation on the ground that it is not specifically characterized.

Support Local Digital Transformation

With smartphones and mobile payment systems spreading across developing Asia and Africa, leading companies are migrating core business processes to affordable, accessible, and smart cloud systems with voice-text interfaces in local languages, strengthening the productivity of the working class.

Decision-support dashboards integrate real-time data from IoT sensors, satellites, and blockchains on logistics flows, infrastructure conditions, and operating environments. That's topped up with AI continuously optimizing predictive freight routing, automated insurance underwriting, customized education, and precision agriculture.

Watch out for Evolving Consumer Preferences

Rapidly growing disposable incomes, the rise of the internet, and the ever-increasing access to external markets have heightened the speed at which lifestyle shifts and consumer sophistication are taking place in all developing nations. This trend is especially notable in the newly bourgeois, greater-youthful, digital-first groups less tied to traditional social mores. STILL HUMAN AFTER ALL.

New offerings require deeper degrees of personal relevance, applications of augmented reality to heighten and dimensionalize, curation enabled by advanced machine learning to introduce curated recommendations, aggregation of price comparisons, and easy financing options. Engaging experiences, available through a limitless digital universe of options, are required to acquire loyalty. HUMANIZATION TAKES BRAND EQUITY FURTHER.

Invest in Talent and Leadership

Ongoing excellence is based on skilled operations leadership experienced in governance success and invested in a regional culture distinct from transactional professionalism. Cultural ownership by long-term residents (versus short-term assignees) resonates with locals.

Training potential future leaders in best practices on a global scale enables the transfer of skills in disciplines such as quality control systems, supply chain analytics, and IP management. Furthermore, leveraging diaspora patriots' natural bridge-building helps to bridge geographical and cultural divides that unknowingly prevent progress. Roadmaps are painstakingly prepared for safe and reliable journeys.

This chapter offers comprehensive strategic guidance tailored to U.S. success-seeking SMBs and startups across six primary domains that are critical to competing in emerging markets: Product Localization and Ongoing Innovation; Understanding Infrastructure Contexts; Focusing on Customer Experiences; Managing Regulatory Environments; and Making Early Moves.

CHAPTER 12: MANAGEMENT BASED ON METRICS AND EMPATHY

Select Key Performance Indicators

To enter an emerging market, have clear key performance indicators (KPIs) set up to track progress. As a U.S. SMB or startup, financial KPIs like revenue growth, profit margins, return on investment, and payback period are critical. However, non-financial KPIs like acquisition, retention, and satisfaction also matter while establishing a new market presence.

Specific KPIs will depend on your objectives. For new market entry, unit sales, new customer sign-ups, app installations, service activations, and other volume metrics indicate market traction. However, low-margin sales won't suffice. Simultaneously monitor average order value, customer lifetime value, referral rates, and churn. Your KPI dashboard lets you balance scale, revenue, and loyalty growth.

Reevaluate KPIs quarterly and adjust for market learnings. Be prepared to experiment with pricing, products, channels, and partnerships if initial KPIs lag. With clear metrics, you can course-correct before overinvesting in a losing strategy.

Track Progress and Adjust Management Accordingly

Connect KPI objectives to market achievements—first local hire, launching a new market, product release, etc. Assign KPIs responsibility by function—sales objectives for sales, user activation for product—to drive accountability. Measure KPIs weekly or monthly, not quarterly, to swiftly react.

Distribute a KPI dashboard with the region and HQ to align priorities. See customer complaints surge? Bolster service capacity. Observe trial drop?

Understand why conversion lags. Find local partnerships not progressing? Obtain executive support. A close call on short-term objectives is permissible if the path to long-term goals still seems plausible. Chronic shortfall against interim objectives indicates fundamental flaws demanding restructuring.

Nuances of a region can mask opportunity. Run on data, but also rely on instinct to judge results. A monthly review should debate whether execution issues or strategy whiffs cause shortfalls. Change timelines, budgets, and teams if the market is undeveloped fully before the exit decision. If in-market metrics don't improve after a concerted campaign, have the guts to exit.

Balance Numbers with a Human Touch

Quantifiable measures drive disciplined management, but people's judgment requires the competence of emotional intelligence. Caring colleagues can camouflage challenges by shadowing virtual teammates from sight. Idiomatic local factors affecting productivity are stranded in translation. Jet-lagged executives flying in every quarter misunderstand every inflection.

Intentionally spend extended periods saturated in native culture - not just flipping through decks in airport lounges. Wander around, watch how people use your products, hang around and chat with the rank and file. Socialize with teammates themselves, not just as workers, but as human beings, with dreams, fears, and families. Numbers mean something only if the people behind them feel respected.

Listen to complaints, gripes and obstinacy. If serious personnel issues are impairing results, have an honest conversation – but always respect the person as a person. In emerging markets, obligations to the clan trump work, so indulge reasonable folks' idiosyncratic needs at need. And trust is no longer confined to transactions only matters more here.

Minimize Office Politics

Complex office politics are spawned in multinational environments when dispersed teams have vague accountabilities. Sales members blame marketing members for poor lead quality. Customer support claims that missed product features are causing escalations. Finance wonders if the headcount is bloated. Diverse personalities and work styles clash. Bruno makes mountains out of molehills. Hal is ego-centric. Bapu ("Acting Like a Big Shot" in Chinese) is unreliable. Vendors and partners stir the pot trying to influence decisions for their benefit.

Diffuse internal tensions by creating clear roles and procedures for conflict resolution. Make sure shared goals trump departmental interests. Codify rules of engagement between functions that describe shared metrics, handoff criteria, escalation processes, etc. Audit major initiatives collectively for sound planning. Convene all parties when addressing complex customer/market/partner needs.

Guard against external parties becoming more fond of some team members than others, providing them privileged access. Demand solid justification for adding vendors or activities. Formalize partner selection & reviews. Openly communicate facts about alternatives. Assign accountability for key decisions to the core team.

Reward Frontline Employees Generously

Frontline sales and service agents represent the primary interface most companies have with emerging market customers. Their product knowledge shapes user experiences directly. Their effort to keep accounts current is directly correlated with the cash flows that grease a company's gears. Their daily grind usually dwarfs the help coming from regional or global office backend support.

Yet frontline workers rarely win recognition relative to strategy-deck drafting managers. Resentment festers when excessive executive awards discount field teams' customer-bearing pressure. Rebalance rewards toward customer-impacting roles. Prefer promotion from within to external executive hiring. Emphasize intrinsic rewards like training, advancement opportunities, and public praise.

Morale and retention erode if employees have the feeling of being undervalued, especially in markets where talent has options. Cement both their loyalty and your reputation on the front lines. Prioritizing their satisfaction can pay off as significantly as getting the key KPIs right.

CHAPTER 13: BE AN HONORABLE CITIZEN

Working in developing countries brings tremendous opportunities for growth, but with it comes social responsibilities. As foreign corporations in these nations, U.S. firms must seek to be exemplary corporate neighbors. This engenders favor with local communities, officials, and business allies. Also, it bolsters public impression and image.

Win Local Market's Respect via Social Responsibility

Companies gain respect and favor by giving back to local communities. While profit is the objective, allocating resources to charitable causes shows real concern. Efforts like teaching work skills, constructing public facilities, sponsoring students, and supplying computers for schools may appear tangential to business, but generate valuable political capital and civic goodwill.

Implement Eco-Friendly Operations to Reduce Total Costs

Another way to be a good citizen is to implement eco-friendly practices in the way we run our facilities and our operations. It makes perfect economic sense in many cases to reduce energy use, water use, materials use, reduce waste, or reduce pollution. And these often have the effect of directly reducing overhead costs. And this is perhaps more important now as environmental regulation tightens as climate change really becomes a major topic globally. So, doing this now has a long-term cost advantage and there is not a lot of compliance risk.

Adopt New Energy Solutions

Insufficient or volatile energy infrastructure is a problem for many developing markets. Power outages hurt productivity, and running on diesel generators is costly and polluting. Renewable energy solutions such as solar panels or wind turbines can offer cleaner, cheaper supplementary power. Although they require some upfront investment, such ideas pay off over time. They also reduce reliance on the grid and exposure to energy price shocks.

Participate in Local Charities and Causes

When a corporation gives money or services to certain defined charities, it is making a statement in two ways: that it cares and that it is not an equal opportunity giver. Causes can be poverty alleviation, health awareness, education access, or disaster relief. This gets the company's name in the paper and across cultural gaps. It doesn't have to be an arm and a leg, but it should be regular, and aligned to corporate values. Employees, incidentally, can be encouraged to donate or volunteer, too.

Respect Local Customs

As you drive change, be careful you don't trample local traditions. Learn key social norms, taboos, dress codes, greetings, dining etiquette and so on. For example, businesses should build around important local holidays and events. The activities of companies should not violate cultural sensitivities either. That respect wins over stakeholders crucial to commercial success.

Source and Hire Locals with Vision

Giving priority to local sourcing and local employment will also bring goodwill. The purchase of local goods is a sign of the community's investment. It is not only saving costs, but also creating jobs and skill training for locals. Do your best to find local suppliers and factories. Source key local personnel including top management positions. If possible, employ and train vulnerable groups. These investments will not be in vain.

Speak the Local Language If Possible

Although English is adequate for business, making an effort to communicate in the native language is an indication of goodwill. Use simple greetings and phrases in business interactions. Translate your signage and documents into a native language. Hire interpreters and translators to help with communication. Language holds societies together —by closing the gap, the foreignness of overseas guests is diminished and a bond can be formed. Don't be surprised at the news videos where many U.S. CEOs take local names to show their alliance with local people and markets.

Share Expertise with Caution

American firms can donate knowledge, training, and technology to make a difference. Deploy employee volunteers to teach at local nonprofits and schools. Blueprint the processes, tools, and systems for public agencies trying to upgrade services. Share field expertise by partnering with universities on curriculum and research. Open-source useful software, biomedical devices, or environmental solutions to extend access. Such knowledge transfers seed progress.

Be Apolitical and Avoiding Controversies

Do not comment on politics in the country in which you are located, even those politics appear undemocratic. Avoid offending authorities or breaking local laws which ban some forms of speech by saying nothing. Do not become embroiled either in the internal divisions of the country or in any of its ethnic tensions. Be totally neutral and concentrate only on business. Exchanges of political observations generally serve no practical purpose.

Follow Regulations Seriously

Make a sincere effort to follow local tax codes, licenses, financial rules, environmental regulations and other laws. Violations, however seemingly minor, can escalate into serious trouble with vindictive officials. Hire consultants and lawyers to keep current with new laws. Consider extra compliance costs the toll of doing business overseas.

Protect Data and Privacy

Pay extra close attention to data security in under-regulated emerging markets. Develop clear policies on what user data is collected and how it is handled. Invest in technology and training to prevent breaches, unwarranted surveillance, and leaks that might trigger a backlash. Build trust by protecting consumer privacy against misuse of data to make money.

Insist Business Integrity

Vigorously protect against improper activities in our own organization. Speak up against accepting bribes, secret commissions, fixing bids, smuggling goods, or slipping gifts to win discretionary treatment. Terminate any employee who violates our ethical sales practices, regardless of rank. Walk the talk on our honesty requirement to prevent negative publicity that could undermine the confidence we have earned from officials, customers, and communities.

Avoid Misleading Marketing

Refrain from making false or confusing assertions in your advertising and promotional materials simply to boost sales quickly. Use your marketing messages to enlighten your customers about your product's good points and limitations, so they can make educated buying choices. Avoid potential customers' disgust through the use of exploitive methods. Instead, develop brand integrity through straightforwardness. The suggestion here is that a loyal customer who was totally satisfied with a purchase will come back for more, and tell others to do the same.

Respect Authorities Despite Disagreements

If you reject a local permit denial, an aggressive tax assessment, or a customs demand as unreasonable, remain businesslike and good-humored during these skirmishes. Avoid intemperate public criticism of their objectionable policies. They're stakeholders too. Never jeopardize access, channels and relationships with key decision-makers over short-term skirmishes. Stay friendly with whoever's calling the shots.

Be a True Partner

Rather than considering the host country as a frontier to be overcome, partners as equals for mutual success. Understand national development priorities and assess company objectives to identify alignment. Help tackle systemic local problems with technology and know-how. Hire and nurture local protégés for senior leadership. Communicate freely the fruits of your research. Seek win-win commercial relationships. View your actions as cultivating a new Silicon Valley, not extracting resources from the hinterlands. One day, competitors will be comrades.

At the core, enlightened self-interest drives responsible corporate conduct; companies manage to profit ethically without destroying local societies and contribute to broader progress. Elevate living standards. Bridge cultural divides. Empower communities. Safeguard environments. Lend authorities a hand where you can. Foster comradeship and trust.

CHAPTER 14: THE LESSONS

Disclaimer: Over the past two decades, our business operations have allowed us to gain the following insights. They have caused more complications than both our organization and our clients anticipated, so we have included them on this list. We present a public case for each point to demonstrate some aspects of the specific risk. This is only for future reference or to share lessons learned during execution.

Recruit a Leader from the Region Who Has Already Won.

Case Brief: An American mobile gaming start-up recruited a local managing director in Southeast Asia who had previously launched multiple consumer apps successfully in the region. His ability to navigate complex regulatory frameworks, market effectively through local channels, and create cultural adaptations was a huge boon to the company's market entry and expansion.

Key Learning: Employing leaders who have a deep understanding of the target market is an investment worth making. The day-to-day, local expertise and networks transform global visions into regional realities.

Professional Skills of Team Members are More Valuable Than Speaking English

Case Brief: When a US robotics company decided to establish a research and development center in Latin America, it made a conscious decision to prioritize hiring smart engineers over fluent English speakers. The company actively recruited from diverse backgrounds and taught them the language and culture. The result was a group of engineers who worked together to solve problems in novel ways, simply because they brought lots of different expertise to collective problem-solving.

Key Learning: In high-growth emerging markets, technical / business capability is far more important than any given language or skill that can be acquired. Effective recruiting for a diverse leadership team begins with a comprehensive search that looks in new places for talent.

Enable Fast Responses and Decisions from HQ

Case Brief: A Middle East–based American manufacturing start-up ran into a roadblock early on. Headquarters took too long to respond to customization requests from local customers, and by the time solutions were approved, the opportunities were gone. The company established a quick-fix process for localized adaptations.

Key Learning: Look for the happy medium between standardized processes and local flexibility. Empower your regional units to make speedier market-adjustment decisions and faster business moves.

Maintain Professional Etiquette

Case in Point: Whilst on a visit to Asia to break into the market, businessmen and women from a US drug company went for a meeting with potential partners dressed in casual shorts and flip-flops. This was judged as disrespectful. The reputational damage could only be addressed with a worldwide PR campaign. The company introduced a cultural training program on professional behavior.

Key Learning: Failure to understand the crucial cultural distinctions before making deals can be the kiss of death. Staff must be made aware of local protocols of etiquette - something that is often neglected – when expanding abroad.

Consultative Sales Approach Is Better for Large Deals

Case in Point: A US-based fleet logistics startup ran a series of sales meetings in the Middle East, leading with a hard-sell, transaction-focused approach. Discovering that many municipalities had systemic issues with their transportation and supply chains; their regional director changed tactics with the goal of working with government agencies to solve their logistics and supply issues first, and sell products. This philosophy change resulted in immediate trust and a national contract.

Key Learning: To sell to institutional customers, especially influential governmental customers, rather than focusing conventional marketing and sales on product and feature sets, you have to lead with macro-level pain and value proposition. Lead with a consultation and find objectives that run alongside your solution, then, and only then, do you position your products and services – there are patient consulting and collaborative relationships to think of.

Blend in Rather Than Stand Out

Case in Point: Instead of heeding the advice of local employees, an American fast food chain decided to enter a conservative Asian market with garish, loud signage that clashed wildly with its understated surroundings. This attracted the attention of the authorities, who put off granting the necessary permits for months as the franchise had to change its look completely, at enormous expense.

Key Learning: Don't differentiate to the extreme without taking the context into account. Locate your brand identity somewhere between maintaining its distinctiveness and making sure it fits in with wherever it is.

Balance Localization and Standardization

Case in Point: A high-end U.S.-based smartphone manufacturer entered the Asian market by offering completely customizable products that met consumers' regionally divergent preferences. However, customization proved so operationally complex that it caused delays to the releases. Instead, the company struck a simpler path, finding a way to balance globally and locally sourced components so that they were flexible enough to address the requirements of top market segments.

Key Learning: Build modular solutions to balance local customization with shared elements for operational efficiency and scale speed to market across multiple regions.

Protection of IP and Data on Your Terms

Case in Point: In an internal communication, the China chief of a U.S. semiconductor producer accused a local JD partner of stealing intellectual property after knockoffs appeared on the market. The charges were stark, straining a vital relationship that competitors subtly cheered. Quieter investigations determined the origin to be a third-party contractor. The executive apologized for rushing to judgment and tried to mend the relationship.

Key Learning: Deal with emerging intellectual property issues with cultural nuance, not reflex. Don't smear entire groups based on the acts of one. Repair relationships even after errors.

Manage with More Patience and Flexibility

Case in Point: The young head of Southeast Asia market entry for a Silicon Valley executive departs in frustration from the all-too-ambitious deadlines and budgets set by HQ that the regional team could never meet. With his direct and Dutch demeanor, he was seen as rude. Ceasing to play the big bully, and adjusting local expectations to market reality frictions were eliminated and performance improved.

Key Learning: Understand the constraints of emerging markets and manage with empathy. Over-management carries a price. Things could get done, but in their own time and costs.

Adopt American Charm in Promotions

Case in Point: Going live with a new brand of beauty products and cosmetics in the United States and the Middle East, the US brand didn't see translation as much of an issue. However, for its first campaign in the Arab world, the brand's team sent a number of advertising and marketing slogans word-for-word through Google. The translations were ludicrous and bewildering, threatening to sink a series of product launches. Thankfully, a local advertising executive came in and saved the day by suggesting Arabic taglines as loquacious as the original American lines. This suggestion saved the campaign and created a legend in Egyptian advertising.

Key Learning: Nothing stops a successful marketing concept, not even poor communication and creativity. Aim to blend successful American marketing concepts with adaptations for resonance in other languages and cultures.

Choose Local Events Carefully

Case in Point: A sustainability-focused business created a biodegradable detergent that was displayed at a superstore's national sales expo in South America. The opportunity was significant even though the expo was crowded, with a visual and auditory cacophony of competitive promotions. Their sustainability-luxe brand identity was not effectively communicated. Owned "pop-up" shops in premium malls were game-changers.

Key Learning: Not all visibility opportunities line up with where a brand wants to go in a new market. Select platforms with care. Customized experiences are everything, proper executions are something else again.

Demand Business Integrity

Case in Point: A quality-control engineer for a U.S. appliance maker in Asia uncovered an unsanctioned third-party substitution in the supply chain. The factory manager confessed. He was using a cheaper part to fatten profits, a common practice in the region. But the corporate president doubled down on his commitment to ethical sourcing. The manager lost his job, the supplier lost its contract. Inspecting of the parts got tougher.

Key Learning: Corruption may be endemic abroad, but not at home. Leaders should set an ethical example while putting up stronger safeguards.

Exercise Caution when Working with Local "Big Shots"

Case in Point: An American consumer goods maker enlisted a famous social media personality in the Middle East to boost relationships with elite socialites through invitation-only affairs. Journalistic exposes ultimately unveiled the socialite's entanglements in litigious situations. There was no monetary loss to speak of, but severing ties immediately to insulate their corporate image hurt their standing with audiences.

Key Learning: Evaluate public image hazards as part of project planning and progress by hiring respected homegrown VIPs. Lay groundwork now so that you're not caught off guard later by your findings even though you have attractive homegrown alternatives now.

Be Careful with the Dollar Exchange Mindset in Spending

Case in Point: During an Asian trade show, the area director authorized overpriced catering which exceeded budgets because the prices seemed low in dollar terms. However, the excessive spending depleted the allotted resources. Converting the limits to values in local currencies made for more prudent stewardship in terms of actual costs.

Key Learning: To avoid distorted decision-making, anchor expense authorizations, forecasts, and variance analyses to budgets accurately converted to local currencies. Think in either currency simultaneously.

Hire an Independent Local Financial Auditor

Case in Point: The Mexican Chief Executive Officer (CEO) of a US-based building materials firm, was sentenced on fraud charges for embezzling funds. After his dismissal, auditors discovered that years of pilferage had gone undetected as a result of weak financial controls by subsidiary finance leadership. The company subsequently established external regional audit teams to tighten independent oversight of its finances, preventing future lapses.

Key Learning: The broader lesson to be drawn from the case is that headquarters cannot exercise financial stewardship of the world's operations from a distance. What must be done is to engage local auditors of good standing and reputation to provide professional assurance and early warning of anomalies.

Treat Government Authorities as Partners, Not Inspectors

Case in Point: A US apparel company employed their Latin American country manager to build relationships with officials, solely to expedite permits and approvals. As luck would have it, minor administrative transgressions resulted in draconian punishments. By connecting with relevant agencies as collaborators, rather than just billpayers, the firm's star government relations employee laid the groundwork for renewals and gave his bosses cover when problems arose.

Key Learning: View government agencies as important partners, not inhibitors. Establishing long-lasting collaborations by keeping these groups valued and involved improved the prospects of support later.

Not Being Paid On Time is a Serious Warning Sign

Case in Point: A consulting company in the US performed public sector agency digital transformation workshops and often dealt with bureaucratic clients around the world who were slow to pay them. In order to decrease the revenue leakages, the company began scaling their invoicing and stopping additional modules until cleared past due payments before the project was wrapped up.

Key Learning: Do not let client payment delays pile up based only on verbal promises from abroad. Establish checkpoints where work only resumes for payment for what has actually been completed.

Use Bilingual, Certified Notary for Important Documents

Case in Point: An indie game development studio failed to have localization agreements notarized in regional jurisdictions and that company is experiencing IP issues with a Chinese publishing partner as a result....fortunately, the original English documents are legally binding- they are controlling contracts. This is an oversight but cases like this are exactly why we need bilingual legal experts to review contracts.

Key Learning: NEVER underestimate the value of registering your contracts formally in the local language through a qualified legal intermediary. The issue of " Lost in the Translation" could cost the company and the local leader.

Brand Alone Does Not Sell

Case in Point: A trendy clothing brand from the USA decided to move into the Middle East, touting its brand cache and social media promotion. When sales fell far below predictions, they looked into why; they had no one concerned with localization, no one to work with Muslim social media and a host of other media problems. The company learned about localization and went through major market research partnering with local influencers, language services, and a host of other localization capabilities to not keep slipping.

Key Learning: Even big brands need a lot of advertising and localization work to become and stay established in emerging markets. Familiarity never sells.

Prices Reasonably

Case in Point: A USA-based e-scooter startup expanding into Asia could adjust ex-USA prices using the raw materials and manufacturing costs in order to reflect market demand. MW was initially sluggish due to high markups, but thorough analyses covering local taxes, duties, marketing dynamics, and competitor benchmarks led to revised competitive pricing which drove volumes.

Key Learning: Avoid arbitrarily raising the prevailing international prices; calculate the total landed costs prudently and price strategically for the target segment's affordability and market intensity.

Create Local Vendor Blacklists

Case in Point: A U.S. MNC in food processing entering a new Asia/Pacific market learned that their ingredient importer was on the regulator's blacklist for quality problems. The local team deftly switched at the last minute, preventing catastrophe; the home office then required thorough background checks on new vendors. The risk from prior and ongoing poor performers well known to authorities but unknown to foreign country partners is real.

Key Learning: Review potential local partners' historical compliance records; merely the absence of apparent problems during preliminary due diligence should not be taken as assurance. Regulator blacklists can add color to an evaluation and address black spots.

These real-world case studies in global pitfalls can provide invaluable learning opportunities for US small- and medium-sized firms and startups looking to avoid common errors when entering emerging markets and managing overseas operations. Applying best practices in leadership, process, risk management, and stakeholder engagement can mean the difference between falling short and succeeding globally. The secret is finding the right balance between operational excellence and cultural nuance in markets that, for all their similarities, remain distinct.

REFERENCES

1. International Monetary Fund. (2022). World Economic Outlook Report.

2. Kharas, H. (2017). The unprecedented expansion of the global middle class. Brookings Institution.

3. Sheth, J. (2020). Impact of emerging markets on marketing. Journal of Marketing, 82(3), 1-6.
U.S. Small Business Administration (2021). International Trade Survey.

4. Engardio, P. (2019). Emerging markets: a gold mine for small businesses. Bloomberg Businessweek.

ACKNOWLEDGEMENT

In the creation of this seminal series, I have had the distinct privilege of drawing upon the invaluable experiences, insights, and expertise generously shared by a distinguished global network of esteemed partners and accomplished friends. Their direct and indirect contributions have been instrumental, and it is with profound gratitude that I acknowledge the indelible influence they have had on this work.

Kanth Krishnan: Managing Director at Accenture, has been a beacon of inspiration with his incisive insights and visionary leadership in technology services. His profound depth of knowledge and innovative approach have significantly enriched the content of this book.

As Managing Director at Newmark, Jeff Pappas has provided critical perspectives on the dynamic global real estate market landscape. His unparalleled expertise has contributed to a deeper understanding of the business environments explored herein.

Mike Beares: Founder and Board Chairman of Clutch.co, has been instrumental in shaping my views on business connectivity through his entrepreneurial spirit and dedication to bridging businesses with the optimal service providers.

Formerly leading Outsourcing and Managed Services at PwC, Charles Aird's comprehensive knowledge and strategic foresight in outsourcing services have greatly contributed to my understanding of this critical business function.

Haitao Qi, Chairman of Devott Research and Advisory, has provided exceptionally enlightening perspectives on technology innovations and market trends, especially in the Asian context.

It has been my great privilege to learn from and collaborate with these distinguished individuals and institutions operating at the leading edge of our industry. Any merits of this book stem directly from the exceptional global network of friends and partners upon whom I rely. Any faults or shortcomings are solely my own.

Last, but unequivocally not least, the unwavering understanding and support of my beloved wife, Biyu, has been an inspiration to this professional endeavor. The intensive writing workload harkened back to my doctoral dissertation at Yale a quarter-century ago. She remains the driving force behind my career growth and personal fulfillment.

ABOUT THE AUTHOR

Stephan S Sunn

Stephan Sunn is the Executive Partner at Sanford Black Advisory, a preeminent global business and investment consultancy. In this capacity, he collaborates with industry leaders to advise companies worldwide on growth strategy, marketing/sales, innovation monetization, partnerships, and mergers & acquisitions. Over the past two decades, Mr. Sunn has consulted on sourcing provider selection for more than 30 international corporations and over 20 investment and M&A deals in the technology services, digital technologies, and global outsourcing sectors.

Mr. Sunn possesses particular expertise in empowering private enterprises to accelerate growth and enhance value creation through engagement with governments and technology parks. He holds a leadership position with Devott Co., China's largest private research firm focused on the IT, software, and technology services industries. Additionally, he serves as a Director at the China IT and Outsourcing Association. His clients span Fortune 500 companies, state-owned enterprises, technology parks, SMBs, and startups in both developed and emerging markets.

A graduate of the University of Science and Technology of China (USTC) with a Bachelor of Science degree, and Yale University with a Master of Science and Ph.D., Mr. Sunn frequently shares his insights and research as a speaker at global conferences and events. He is a prolific author and an accomplished presenter for his projects and clients around the world.

Contact: Stephan.sunn@aya.yale.edu | Tel: 17046521119 | Whatsapp: 17247891898

www.ingramcontent.com/pod-product-compliance
Lightning Source LLC
Chambersburg PA
CBHW050325230526
45471CB00005B/2360